TRUCKS & OFF-ROAD VEHICLES

TRUCKS & OFF-ROAD VEHICLES

General Editor:
Richard Gunn

MOTORBOOKS

This edition published in 2006 by Motorbooks, an imprint of MBI Publishing Company, Galtier Plaza, Suite 200, 380 Jackson Street, St. Paul, MN 55101-3885 USA

MBI Publishing Company titles are also available at discounts in bulk quantity for industrial or sales-promotional use. For details write to Special Sales Manager at MBI Publishing Company, Galtier Plaza, Suite 200, 380 Jackson Street, St. Paul, MN 55101-3885 USA

ISBN-13: 978-0-7603-2569-8
ISBN-10: 0-7603-2569-3

Produced by
Amber Books Ltd
Bradley's Close
74–77 White Lion Street
London N1 9PF
www.amberbooks.co.uk

Printed in Singapore

All photographs © International Masters Publishers AB except 6, 8–10, 12, 13, 15: TRH/Cody Images; 11: Giles Chapman Library

This material was previously published as part of the reference set Hot Cars

CONTENTS

Introduction

Off-roaders, sports utility vehicles, pickups, recreational vehicles, light trucks, 4x4s, general purpose vehicles. Call them what you will, it's now difficult to imagine the modern motoring scene without these big, blocky vehicles dominating city centers, countryside roads, and agricultural tracks.

Like 'em or loathe 'em—and there seem to be approximately equal numbers in each camp—sports utility vehicles (SUVs) and their close pickup relations have enjoyed an unprecedented level of popularity in recent years. The closing decade of the 20th and the dawn of the 21st century have seen huge growth in the SUV and light truck marketplace, outstripping demand for more conventional, less versatile car formats. By a combination of accident and clever marketing, what were once specialist vehicles have now become commonplace sights, many being bought on the basis of their imposing looks rather than for their original all-terrain abilities.

Despite mounting opposition from environmental and safety groups, SUVs and light trucks look like they're here to stay, and these mobile bunkers on wheels with true 'go-anywhere, do-anything' capabilities are likely to be around for a very long time to come.

Tough and practical

The vehicles in this book fall into two general categories. Firstly, there are the utilitarian workhorses: two-wheel and four-wheel drive vehicles built strictly to serve. They are typified by the British Land Rover and the original U.S. Jeep and Ford F-series pickups. Resilient, dependable, and capable of taking any amount of punishment while still faithfully performing their duties, their hardy characteristics have won them millions of

The Ford F-1 of 1948 was the mother of the long-running F-series of pickups. The range is now an American legend... and the trucks have grown a lot bigger since the 1940s!

fans and earned them almost iconic status in their homelands. Indeed, in 2003, the Land Rover was voted the greatest vehicle ever built in a British television viewers poll. Granted, the nation that spawned the affectionately nicknamed 'Landie' might be expected to vote for its own ahead of foreign rivals. But it also beat off such tough opposition as the Jaguar E-type and Rolls-Royce Silver Cloud, both beautiful, luxurious, faster, and much more expensive than the Land Rover. Not bad for a primitive yet effective piece of technology born in the 1940s and intended just as a temporary stopgap in the Rover car range. The fact that the Land Rover won, and that it still remains in production today as the Defender, is a testament to how much respect and admiration it has earned over the last half century.

Away from Britain, the American and Australian love affair with the pickup has endured for the best part of a century, and for those who have relied upon them for their livelihood, these robust vehicles have played as important a role as the horse did in the days before mechanization. They contributed to opening up some of the more geographically challenging parts of these two young nations during the last half century, and helped make it possible for people to survive and prosper in areas that would otherwise have been too hostile. Modern America owes much to the pickup, and Australia has the same debt of gratitude to what it has come to christen the "ute."

Urban 4WD luxury

Secondly, you'll find SUVs, the flipside of the coin. These vehicles owe their existence to vehicles like the Land Rover and the Jeep, but their nature is very different indeed. Invariably all-wheel drive, they combine cross-country ability with luxury and are designed to be just as comfortable off the road as they are on it. In America, the Jeep Corporation (and its various owners) was a pioneer in this field,

An example of the new breed of SUV, the Dodge Durango combines trucklike strength and size with carlike comfort, ride and handling.

gradually developing its original wartime fighting machine into something more palatable for civilian tastes. But it was Britain that popularized the concept. From the Land Rover was born the Range Rover of 1970, a more refined version that possessed much of the Landie's versatility and skill, yet didn't forget that looks and frills were important as well. It spawned a host of imitations, and few auto firms these days, whether American, European or Asian, don't now offer some sort of high-spec 4x4, including some companies that once used to deride such vehicles. Even some of the most exotic European marques like Porsche and Lamborghini have got in on the all-wheel act, with the Cayenne and LM-002 respectively. How long might it be until the likes of Ferrari, Aston Martin, or even Rolls-Royce join them? Stranger things have happened.

Europe and the Far East may not have embraced the philosophy of the pickup truck in quite the same way as America and Australia have done, but enthusiasm for SUVs is global. You'll find many examples of the breed, such as the Toyota Land Cruiser, Isuzu Trooper, Chrysler Jeep Grand Cherokee and the old favourite Range Rover everywhere and anywhere in the world. From New York, London, or Paris to the remotest wilds of Africa or Australia, SUVs are perfectly at home, whatever the environment might inflict on them.

Designer pickups
Alongside these two main types, we've thrown in some oddities as well, just to prove that anything can happen with these kinds of machines, and often does. For example, there's the glorious 1959 Chevrolet El Camino, a pickup truck based on one of the most flamboyant cars ever built. Created from the most ostentatious Chevy of all time, the batwing-finned '59 Impala, the El Camino dripped chrome and topped off its open load area at the

rear with the same dramatic fins as on the road car. Who cared that anybody buying one would have been too afraid to give it any hard work for fear of denting all that glitter or scratching the paintwork? It looked amazing, and for some that was more important than what it actually did. Working machines have rarely been cooler, and there hasn't been anything like it since.

A further variation on the principle of mad pickups was Dodge's Li'l Red Express truck, made for just two years from 1978 to 1979. With government regulations strangling horsepower in passenger cars but leaving so-called utility vehicles alone, Dodge chose to sneakily spice things up a bit and effectively built a muscle car disguised as a pickup. Available in any colour, so long as it was scarlet of course, the Li'l Red Express had a top speed of almost 120mph, and could out-accelerate a Porsche 911 and a Ferrari 308GTS. It eventually became

If it looks a bit like a Jeep, that's because the Land Rover was inspired by the US Army's WWII workhorse. Over half a century later, it's still noticeably related to the 1948 original.

known as the last American hotrod, giving a completely new meaning to the term 'express delivery!' Like the El Camino 20 years before it, it was a radical interpretation of an established idea, and extraordinary for its day. Both of these vehicles can be regarded as among the first of the 'designer' pickups, fashionable vehicles based on conventional ideas with a none-too-subtle twist. Such machines are now becoming popular once again.

Truck development
In the timeline of 4x4s, pickups and SUVs, it's the truck that came first. Man invented the wheel not to carry himself, but to move heavy loads. Most developments of the wheel, such as the horse and

Top: Land Rovers could be made a bit more hospitable with the addition of a hardtop, but roof or no roof they were still very spartan creations.

Bottom: A current Range Rover doing what it still does best: getting dirty in difficult conditions. Combining luxury and cross-country performance was a novel idea in 1970, however.

cart or railways, placed the emphasis on shifting goods first, and then transporting people almost as an afterthought. The car was an exception to this rule. The first primitive automobiles of the 1880s were solely passenger vehicles, but it didn't take long before the possibilities of the internal combustion engine were realized by those wanting to move around items a little heavier than the average human being. The car was still a fad when the coachbuilders started producing pickup bodies for fitting onto existing chassis. As is so often the way with new technology, it was military need that gave the breed added impetus.

World War I was the first major mechanized conflict in history, and trucks played a key role in the hostilities. Before the war was over, two of the three biggest names in American pickups had built their first models. Dodge started manufacturing trucks in 1917, Chevrolet followed in 1918, the year it became part of General Motors. The third force, Ford, was a late starter, and it wasn't until 1925 that it introduced its first factory-produced example, based on the Model T. It soon made up for lost time with its F-series, launched

in 1948, which went on to become one of America's biggest sellers in any automotive category. The Big Three have been responsible for millions of pickups, sold not just in America, but across the world. Australia, almost as vast and difficult in terrain as the US, was one of the biggest export markets until its own pickup industry became established.

Four wheels good...

Appearing around the same time as the pickup was four-wheel drive. Although an all-wheel-driven steam carriage had been built in Britain in 1824, it wasn't until 1898 that the French manufacturer Latil applied the principles to the automobile in the search for greater traction. It is Ferdinand Porsche who is credited as the father of modern 4x4, which makes Porsche's recent excursion into SUVs somehow more understandable. The 25-year-old

In many ways, the AM General Hummer is the Willys Jeep of the modern world. Developed for the US military in the 1980s, the civilian version pictured followed in 1992. It may not be quite as tough, but it's just as impressive!

Japanese SUVs have become universally popular in recent decades. Toyota's Land Cruiser is one of the most successful examples of four-wheel drive technology from the Far East.

engineer invented a system with electric hub motors on each wheel in 1900, with the engine running a dynamo for power supply. Its principles would soon be superseded (although NASA did later borrow the idea for its moon buggy) but it was Porsche's early vision that provided the basis for others to develop. By 1902, the Dutch firm of Spyker had built the first full-time four-wheel-drive car, and FWD manufactured the first American 4x4 in 1911, later supplying both American and British forces during World War I.

It was World War II that produced the most famous four-wheel-drive of them all, however. The Willys Jeep was hurriedly prepared to meet the US Army's requirement for a light reconnaissance vehicle also capable of providing infantry support. Almost 650,000 of these basic military machines were built between 1941 and 1945, proving an priceless weapon in the Allied arsenal. According to General Dwight D. Eisenhower, there were

three tools that won the war: the Dakota transport plane, the landing craft, and the Jeep. Praise indeed. And if imitation is the sincerest form of flattery, then the Jeep was paid a huge compliment by the Land Rover of 1948. Maurice Wilkes, chief engineer of the Rover car company in Britain had an army surplus Jeep on his farm. Recognizing its innovative qualities, he decided that Rover should build an imitator to temporarily see it through the austere years that followed the end of the war. Well over 50 years later, the Land Rover has arguably become a greater motoring icon than the Jeep it took for its inspiration.

Birth of the SUV
The genesis of the SUV is more difficult to pin down. The consensus of opinion among motoring historians is that it can be traced back to the 'depot hacks' of the 1920s, used for transporting passengers and luggage from railway stations. They were commonly known as Carryalls or Suburbans, and as well as giving birth to the SUV, they also spawned the modern station wagon/estate car. These origins of the species were meant to be

purely practical, and, as the nickname suggested, intended to carry all, whether people or goods. Perhaps the first genuine SUV, under the modern interpretation of the term, was the Willys Jeep Wagon of the late 1940s, actually advertised as the 'utility vehicle for the family.' It was seen as a useful but fun all-purpose transport, to complement or even replace the usual family car.

Again, it was the Jeep Corporation that continued to lead the way in America, but it was Rover that fine-tuned the SUV and set down the rules for what would follow. During the 1960s, the company had noticed that the leisure market for Land Rovers was growing faster than the agricultural and military sides, and that over in the United States many 4x4 vehicles were being used purely for recreational purposes. With Rover's considerable expertise and reputation in cross-country engineering, it was a wonderful opportunity to come up with something different.

Although its notion of an 'upmarket' Land Rover was a simple one, the Range Rover of 1970 was more than just a Landie with a new engine and a few comfy cushions scattered inside. It was completely new in every way, and totally revolutionary too. There was simply nothing like it at the time, although once other auto makers saw how successful it was, they soon rushed to build their own. The SUV market was established, and grew rapidly.

21st century trucks and SUVs
Today, pickups are still bought to carry tough loads, SUVs are still purchased for their off-roading abilities. But now, more than ever before, these

The Jeep's contribution to the Allied war effort during World War II was immeasurable. Little could stop this motorized version of the cavalry horse, whether it was up against tough terrain or enemy fire.

Above: Ford F-series trucks are tough enough as it is, but some owners have to go even further. This F-350 has been customized to make it even more unstoppable.

Right: Isuzu's cross-country mud-plugger, in all its various incarnations, has forged a reputation for reliability and capability. This is a second-generation 1984 model.

vehicles are fashion statements. They're bought by people who have little intention of ever going cross-country, or using the load area of a truck for anything more challenging than heavy shopping or a new television set. These imposing, seemingly indestructible machines give owners a sense of invulnerability on increasingly crowded and dangerous modern roads. Owners feel safe and secure inside, sitting high above other traffic and insulated from everything that makes modern driving so demanding. They also feel at the forefront of automotive technology and styling.

Despite those who claim that tall and bulky vehicles are dangerous for other drivers who own smaller cars, and environmentally unfriendly because they consume too much fuel, when it comes to motoring cool, there's little that can eclipse an SUV or a big pickup. Trends may come and go, and designs may change to reflect the times, but these species show no real signs of losing their popularity in the near future. This book explores how these basic utilitarian workhorses gradually metamorphosed into some of the most desirable vehicles of the early 21st century.

AM General HUMMER

Built for the military, and one of the stars of the Gulf Wars, the massive go-anywhere, over-anything off-roader—originally known as a Humvee— has become a cult vehicle guaranteed to get you noticed anywhere.

"... Unstoppable off-roader."

"You're cocooned high above traffic in your Hummer feeling an enormous sense of security and take-on-anything confidence. The ride is softer than you imagine, but its sheer bulk makes it awkward on normal roads—as does its lethargic performance—and the noise at highway speeds batters you. None of this matters off-road, though, where the Hummer shrinks around you and really comes into its own. Poor flat-out performance becomes irrelevant because this unstoppable off-roader will ford rivers and climb mountains all day long."

Because of the huge transmission tunnel, the Hummer is not as spacious as you might expect.

Milestones

1980 AM General's version of the High Mobility Multi-purpose Wheeled Vehicle (HMMWV) starts tests in the Nevada desert, just 11 months after design work began.

1983 U.S. Army orders 55,000 HMMWVs, to be delivered in the following five years. The clumsy title is soon modified to Humvee just so it can be spoken. The Humvees would be produced in more than a dozen different versions. It could be bodied as an armored car, personnel carrier or ambulance.

Long suspension travel helps off-road traction.

1992 Sales to the public begin after a lot of publicity is generated by seeing the Humvees in the Gulf War.

1994 Original Chevy 350-cubic inch gasoline V8 is supplanted by the new 378-cubic inch GM diesel V8 engine with little change to the power output.

1996 Hummer buyers now have a choice of normally aspirated or turbo diesel engines and the range comprises seven variants, including a five-door, two- and four-door pickups and a four-door convertible, available from 40 dealers across the US.

UNDER THE SKIN

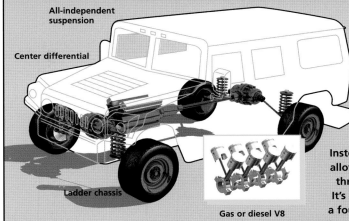

All-independent suspension

Center differential

Ladder chassis

Gas or diesel V8

Hang tough

The Hummer was built to be military tough—weight was not an issue so there's a massive ladder-type frame under the slab-sided body. Its go-anywhere role meant traditional off-roaders' live axles were not chosen. Instead, an all-independent system allows enormous ground clearance through the center of the vehicle. It's all-wheel drive, of course, with a four-speed auto transmitting to a two-speed transfer case and center differential.

THE POWER PACK

Gasoline or diesel?

Hummers started with the 350-cubic inch Chevrolet small-block V8 (shown). In the Hummer, it was tuned for torque rather than outright power. In 1994, it switched to GM's bigger 395-cubic inch V8 diesel as standard. It's a development of the 387-cubic inch diesel produced for GM by its Detroit Diesel Division and it is designed with turbocharging very much in mind. The turbocharged version of the big diesel, launched in the late-1990s, gained another 10 bhp, and up to 430 lb-ft of stump-pulling torque.

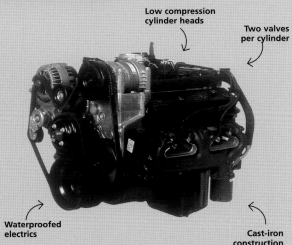

Low compression cylinder heads

Two valves per cylinder

Waterproofed electrics

Cast-iron construction

No stopping it

It's heavy and it's slow. Conventional pick-up trucks at half the price can carry more and go much faster. However, with 430 lb-ft of torque at 1,700 rpm there's no other off-roader that can get you over more rugged mountains or through deeper rapids than a Hummer.

There's nowhere you can't go in a Hummer.

AM General **HUMMER**

Intimidated by Peterbilts and Kenworths? If you want to get on more equal terms without going the whole 18-wheeler route, get yourself a Hummer. Just don't get upset when the trucks still go faster.

Turbocharged option

One of the engine options is a turbocharged version of the 395-cubic inch diesel. It only produces an extra 10 bhp, but adds a great amount of torque which is what the heavyweight Hummer needs to move it along.

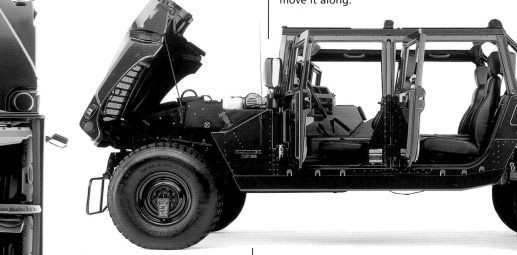

Two-speed transfer case

With a two-speed transfer case to give low and high ratio gears, there are eight forward gears available and a gear for every situation. The Hummer also uses advanced Torsen differentials in the front and rear.

Separate chassis

Because it was intended to have many different bodies fitted to it, the basic Hummer structure had to be a traditional ladder-type chassis rather than a unitary monocoque structure.

Independent suspension

To allow high ground clearance and better individual wheel articulation, the Hummer has all-around independent suspension instead of the usual live rear axle arrangement employed by most off-roaders.

Enormous ground clearance

Hummers ride high, with an excellent 16-inch ground clearance, helped by the independent suspension design which allows 9.1 inches of suspension travel on each wheel.

Extra wide

As a military vehicle, the Hummer wasn't designed to fit on the road, so it could be made very wide, making it stable even with that high ground clearance. How wide is it? At 86.5 inches it's 13.8 inches wider than a full-size Chevrolet sedan.

No overhangs

The wheelbase is almost as long as the vehicle itself. This wheel-at-each-corner design means there's nothing to get in the way when the Hummer climbs and descends. It has an excellent approach angle of 73 degrees.

Diesel V8

Although the Hummer started out with GM's small-block Chevy V8 gasoline engine the larger 395-cubic inch, GM diesel—used in the Chevrolet Tahoe and GMC Yukon—was added to the series as the standard powerplant in the mid-1990s.

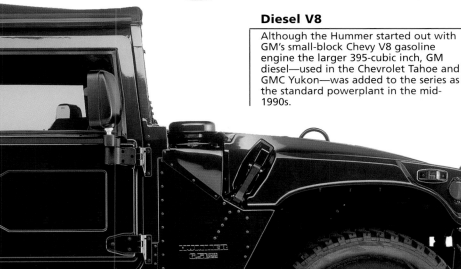

Specifications
1997 AM General Hummer

ENGINE
Type: V8 diesel
Construction: Cast-iron block and heads
Valve gear: Two valves per cylinder operated by single block-mounted camshaft via pushrods, rockers and hydraulic lifters
Bore and stroke: 4.06 in. x 3.82 in.
Displacement: 395 c.i.
Compression ratio: 21.5:1
Induction system: Electronic fuel injection with turbocharger
Maximum power: 195 bhp at 3,400 rpm
Maximum torque: 430 lb-ft at 1,700 rpm
Top speed: 87 mph
0–60 mph: 17.3 sec.

TRANSMISSION
Four-speed GM 4L80-E automatic with two-speed transfer case and center differential; four-wheel drive with Torsen differentials

BODY/CHASSIS
Steel ladder frame with choice of five bodies

SPECIAL FEATURES

The optional tire inflation/deflation system enables you to drop the tire pressure for extra traction in slippery off-road conditions, then reinflate them automatically to their standard pressures. Each tire costs $500, though.

Front and rear tow hooks come standard so Hummer drivers can easily pull humbler vehicles from mud or snow.

RUNNING GEAR
Steering: Power-assisted recirculating ball
Front suspension: Unequal length wishbones, coil springs, telescopic shocks and anti-roll bar
Rear suspension: Unequal length wishbones, coil springs and telescopic shocks
Brakes: Vented discs front and rear
Wheels: Steel discs 8.3 in. x 16.5 in.
Tires: 37 in. x 12.5 in. R16.5

DIMENSIONS
Length: 184.5 in.   **Width:** 86.5 in.
Height: 72 in.   **Wheelbase:** 130 in.
Track: 72 in. (front and rear)
Weight: 6,620 lbs.

Chevrolet 3100 STEPSIDE

Since the day they were introduced, the 1955-1957 Chevy® 3100 series trucks have always been hugely popular. They make great custom haulers, too, as witnessed by the thousands of them on the roads.

"...stylish and dependable."

"The door swings on vault-like hinges and closes with reassuring firmness. It may look stylish, but this truck is still dependable to the core. The big bench seat takes you back to the 1950s, but the digital instruments are right up to date. A torquey small-block under the hood moves you along with a constant flow of power from its tri-power carburetors. The ride is fairly good for an old truck and modern tires keep it in line even on the most slippery roads."

By 1957, Chevy pickups were becoming more and more carlike, inside and out.

Milestones

1955 In March, Chevrolet

unveils a new line of light-duty trucks. These are offered with a ½- to 1-ton carrying capacity. Big news is a new overhead-valve V8 engine and the 3100 Cameo™, a deluxe ½-ton pickup with a long box, slab-sided bed and deluxe trim. Only 5,219 of these are built.

The previous Bullnose 3100 lasted from 1948 until 1954.

1956 Styling is virtually

unchanged this year save for a new hood ornament, but engine tweaks result in an extra 17 bhp on the standard six, and power is up to 205 bhp from the four-barrel V8.

Most expensive of the 3100 series in 1957 was the Cameo.

1957 A flatter hood with

twin bullets and a new grill with a center loop mark the major changes. Four-wheel drive Chevrolet pickups are offered for the first time.

UNDER THE SKIN

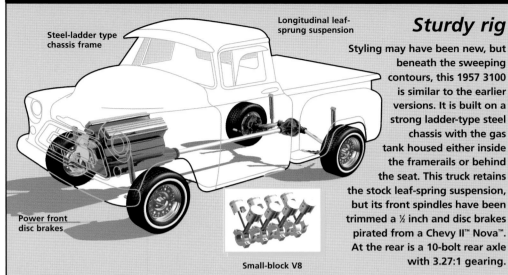

Steel-ladder type chassis frame

Longitudinal leaf-sprung suspension

Power front disc brakes

Small-block V8

Sturdy rig

Styling may have been new, but beneath the sweeping contours, this 1957 3100 is similar to the earlier versions. It is built on a strong ladder-type steel chassis with the gas tank housed either inside the framerails or behind the seat. This truck retains the stock leaf-spring suspension, but its front spindles have been trimmed a ½ inch and disc brakes pirated from a Chevy II™ Nova™. At the rear is a 10-bolt rear axle with 3.27:1 gearing.

THE POWER PACK

Sports car power

In 1955, Chevrolet released its infamous 265-cubic inch, small-block V8. This small block would vary from size to size, but the basic block has been used for more than five decades now. This 1957 3100 came from the factory with V8 power, but where the original 165-bhp mill once sat, there is now a 1970 Corvette® 350. It has been mildly tweaked with a free-flowing aluminum intake and three Rochester two-barrel carburetors, a late-model MSD ignition system and a heavy-duty alternator. It currently produces a streetwise 330 bhp at 5,200 rpm and a strong 360 lb-ft of torque. This makes the truck easy to drive, but also incredibly quick off the line.

Choice Chevy

Some of the most stylish pickups built during the mid-1950s are the the 3100 series. They are collectors' and enthusiasts' favorites today. Many have been turned into modified drivers that are high on looks, performance and practicality, too.

A 1957 hot-rodded Stepside is a popular choice for those who modify trucks.

Chevrolet **3100 STEPSIDE**

Classic styling combined with detailed yet subtle touches makes this 3100 Series a real head-turner on the street. With some serious power under the hood, this truck is a performer as well as a first-rate looker.

Mighty Mouse engine

Nicknamed the Mouse, the small-block Chevy V8's abundance and simplicity made it the first choice of power for hot-rodders. This 1957 truck has a 350-cubic inch version from 1970.

Class designation

In 1957, Chevrolet light-duty trucks were offered in a variety of forms depending on their carrying capacity. The smallest (3100) was certified for 5,000 lbs. GVW while bigger 3442/3542 and 3742 series trucks could haul up to 7000 lbs. With its varnished wood bed, this truck is more for showing than hauling.

Turbo 350 automatic

As one of the best automatic transmissions ever built, the TH350 was a mainstay of GM cars and trucks during the 1970s and is one of the most reliable units ever made.

Stepside bed

While the classy Cameo got a slab-sided bed with unique taillights and trim, other 3100s stuck with the traditional, for the time, stepside bed. Custom truck builders today tend to prefer the look of the nostalgic stepside bed.

Chrome trim

Back in the 1980s, body color and blackout trim were all the rage, though today, chrome has made a comeback on the custom scene. Chromed C-pillars, floor bed brackets, and side steps add to this truck's appeal.

Old and new interior

Inside this Chevy is a mixture of both old and new. A traditional-style bench seat is retained, as are the stock door panels and dash. A leather-wrapped, thick-rimmed steering wheel and digital gauges are modern touches.

Raked stance

Many street trucks have dropped front ends to give a tough look. On examples like this one with leaf-springs, it is achieved by cutting the front spindles.

Car-derived styling

With trucks beginning to move into the personal transportation sector during the 1950s, the 1955-1957 3100 trucks took many cues from regular passenger cars, including the swept-forward fenders and wraparound windshield.

Specifications

1957 Chevrolet 3100 Stepside

ENGINE

Type: V8

Construction: Cast-iron block and heads

Valve gear: Two valves per cylinder operated by a single centrally-mounted camshaft via pushrods and rockers

Bore and stroke: 4.00 in. x 3.48 in.

Displacement: 350 c.i.

Compression ratio: 10.25:1

Induction system: Three Rochester two-barrel carburetors

Maximum power: 330 bhp at 5,200 rpm

Maximum torque: 360 lb-ft at 3,400 rpm

Top speed: 115 mph

0–60 mph: 7.2 sec.

TRANSMISSION

GM TH350 three-speed automatic

BODY/CHASSIS

Steel ladder-type chassis with steel cab and pickup bed

SPECIAL FEATURES

1957 Chevy trucks have a unique one-year-only, loop-style grill.

Chromed Chevrolet lettering on the tailgate adds a touch of class.

RUNNING GEAR

Steering: Recirculating ball

Front suspension: Beam axle, with semi-elliptic leaf springs and telescopic shock absorbers

Rear suspension: Live axle, with semi-elliptic leaf springs and telescopic shock absorbers

Brakes: Discs (front), drums (rear)

Wheels: Centerline 7 x 14 in.

Tires: BF Goodrich radial 205/75/R14

DIMENSIONS

Length: 185.7 in.   **Width:** 69.6 in.

Height: 75.5 in.   **Wheelbase:** 114.0 in.

Track: 57.3 in. (front), 56.4 in. (rear)

Weight: 3,230 lbs.

Chevrolet **C10**

Chevrolet trucks have always been popular workhorses, but with the advent of a new C/K series in the 1970s, they began to take on a different role as family hauler or tricked out street machine.

"...a serious muscle truck."

"This generation of C/K series has a much improved cabin, with a better dash layout and more space. The bench seat may be utilitarian, but starting the big-block rat motor soon erases any feelings of a work truck. The V8 is a torque monster at low rpm and enables you to out perform many late model performance cars. With dual exhaust, the sound is truly awesome and lets any challenger know that this is a serious muscle truck."

The interior has been upgraded with many machined aluminum trim pieces.

Milestones

1973 General Motors launches

a new generation of full-size trucks, which are larger and more spacious than their predecessors. Also joining them are a redesigned Blazer® sport utility and Suburban®. Both the engines and chassis are carried over from the previous models.

The featured truck uses a 454-V8 from a Corvette®.

1978 There are

minor improvements to the interior of the big trucks.

1979 All full-size

trucks are fitted with a catalytic convertor and require unleaded fuel. The hood and grill treatment are also altered.

An all-new Chevy® half-ton pickup made its debut for 1988.

1981 Both the Chevrolet C/K and GMC®

Sierra® get a new front grill with square, stacked headlights. Electronic spark control is added to the small-block V8.

UNDER THE SKIN

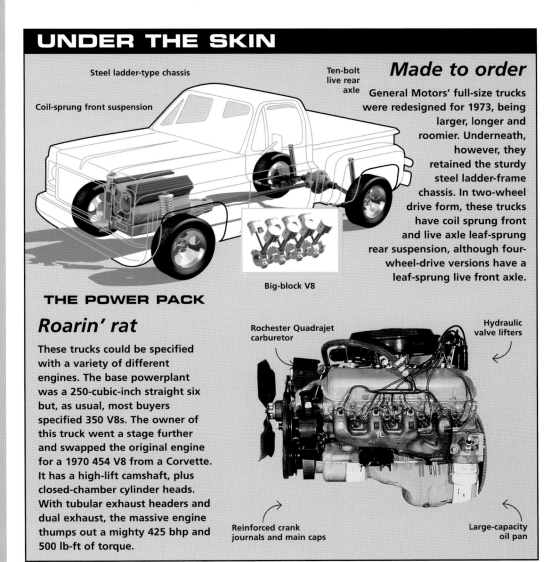

Steel ladder-type chassis

Coil-sprung front suspension

Ten-bolt live rear axle

Big-block V8

Made to order

General Motors' full-size trucks were redesigned for 1973, being larger, longer and roomier. Underneath, however, they retained the sturdy steel ladder-frame chassis. In two-wheel drive form, these trucks have coil sprung front and live axle leaf-sprung rear suspension, although four-wheel-drive versions have a leaf-sprung live front axle.

THE POWER PACK

Roarin' rat

These trucks could be specified with a variety of different engines. The base powerplant was a 250-cubic-inch straight six but, as usual, most buyers specified 350 V8s. The owner of this truck went a stage further and swapped the original engine for a 1970 454 V8 from a Corvette. It has a high-lift camshaft, plus closed-chamber cylinder heads. With tubular exhaust headers and dual exhaust, the massive engine thumps out a mighty 425 bhp and 500 lb-ft of torque.

Rochester Quadrajet carburetor

Hydraulic valve lifters

Reinforced crank journals and main caps

Large-capacity oil pan

Stepside

Because of its small bed, it wasn't very utilitarian when new. Today, the half-ton Stepside has become a popular truck to modify. Rugged construction and huge engine bays make it an ideal street machine They are also easy to build and modify.

The Stepside version is the preferred C10 for street duty.

25

Chevrolet **C10**

Its chunky styling still looks almost contemporary, and the tasteful and subtle modifications give little indication that underneath its meek exterior, this is a killer street pickup.

Big-block V8

Although C10s use 350 cubic-inch small-block engines, this one has a 1970 Corvette 454-cubic inch mill. With high-flowing heads and an aggressive cam, this pickup can cover the ¼-mile in 15.8 seconds.

TurboHydramatic transmission

Due to the incredible torque from the 454 V8, an equally stout transmission is required. This Chevy is fitted with a tough TurboHydramatic 400 three-speed automatic with a 1,800-rpm stall speed torque convertor and shift kit.

Aftermarket wheels

No custom pickup is complete without a set of aftermarket wheels. In keeping with the period look, this Chevy rides on slotted Western cast-aluminum wheels, shod in modern Goodyear Eagle GT performance tires.

Square styling

The 1973 Chevy and GMC trucks differed considerably from the 1967-1972 models. The later versions have bulkier squared off styling. In fact, this redesign proved so successful and popular that it lasted in various guises until 1992.

Stepside bed

Although the Fleetside style was the most popular, hot rodders seem to prefer the narrow bed and large rear fenders of the Stepside models.

Billet grill

Another popular modification on these trucks is to replace the stock grill assembly with billet-style mesh.

vered suspension

opular modification on
et pickups is to lower
suspension. On this
-wheel drive C10, the
-sprung front has been
pped four inches,
le the rear has been
ered by 3½ inches.

Dual exhaust

A full-length dual exhaust system is usually the first modification done to a street machine. This truck uses a dual 2½ inch diameter system to quickly release the engine's exhaust. It lets out a great bellow in the process.

Specifications

1974 Chevrolet C10

ENGINE

Type: V8

Construction: Cast-iron block and heads

Valve gear: Two valves per cylinder operated by pushrods and rockers

Bore and stroke: 4.25 in. x 4.0 in.

Displacement: 454 c.i.

Compression ratio: 10.25:1

Induction system: Rochester Quadrajet four-barrel carburetor

Maximum power: 425 bhp at 6,200 rpm

Maximum torque: 500 lb-ft at 3,400 rpm

Top speed: 122 mph

0–60 mph: 7.8 sec.

TRANSMISSION

GM TurboHydramatic three-speed automatic

BODY/CHASSIS

Steel cab and bed on separate steel ladder-type chassis

SPECIAL FEATURES

The engine bay has been dressed up with chrome valve covers, air cleaner and radiator support.

The original wood floor has been replaced with finished oak boards.

RUNNING GEAR

Steering: Recirculating ball

Front suspension: Unequal-length wishbones with coil springs

Rear suspension: Live axle with semi-elliptic leaf springs and telescopic shock absorbers

Brakes: Discs (front), drums (rear)

Wheels: Western cast-aluminum, 8 x 15 in. (front), 10 x 15 in. (rear)

Tires: Goodyear Eagle, P225/60 R15 (front), P275/60 R15 (rear)

DIMENSIONS

Length: 182.6 in.   **Width:** 80.4 in.

Height: 61.7 in.   **Wheelbase:** 117.5 in

Track: 67.5 in. (front), 68.2 in. (rear)

Weight: 4,045 lbs.

Chevrolet EL CAMINO

It isn't a car and it isn't a pick-up. The idea was to combine the luxury, comfort, and style of the 1959 Chevrolets with the convenience and practicality of a large and handy load bed.

"...more car than truck."

"When driving the El Camino without the optional heavy-duty springs and with a load on board, you'll realize it's more car than truck as it bottoms over even small bumps. With a ride that is both soft and comfortable, the driver must take care through the turns. The steering takes a lot of effort, requiring six turns lock-to-lock. When fitted with one of the optional big-block V8 engines the El Camino's performance is outstanding, although traction is poor."

The interiors of 1959 El Caminos were typical of most cars from the late 1950s.

Milestones

1958 Launched as

a 1959 model in response to Ford's fast-selling Ranchero, the El Camino is based on the full-size Chevy wagon. Top-of-the-line models are extremely fast and can be fitted with an optional Corvette close-ratio four-speed transmission.

The similarity of the El Camino and the Chevrolet Impala is clear to see.

1959 Despite a minor restyle, sales fall

by over a quarter in the 1960 model year to a figure that is unacceptable to Chevrolet.

Over the years, a popular modification is dropping an El Camino body on a 4x4 chassis.

1960 There is no place for the El Camino in

the 1961 model year line; poor sales have doomed it to extinction.

1964 Chevrolet decides that the El Camino

concept is worth reviving and produces a new model based on the sporty mid-size Chevelle.

UNDER THE SKIN

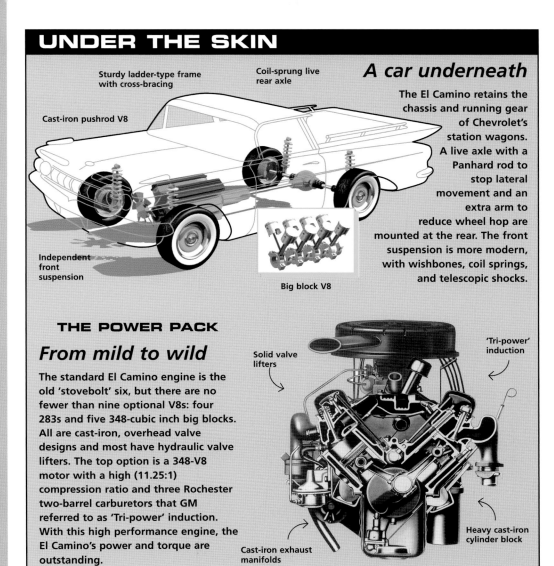

Sturdy ladder-type frame with cross-bracing

Coil-sprung live rear axle

Cast-iron pushrod V8

Independent front suspension

Big block V8

A car underneath

The El Camino retains the chassis and running gear of Chevrolet's station wagons. A live axle with a Panhard rod to stop lateral movement and an extra arm to reduce wheel hop are mounted at the rear. The front suspension is more modern, with wishbones, coil springs, and telescopic shocks.

THE POWER PACK

From mild to wild

The standard El Camino engine is the old 'stovebolt' six, but there are no fewer than nine optional V8s: four 283s and five 348-cubic inch big blocks. All are cast-iron, overhead valve designs and most have hydraulic valve lifters. The top option is a 348-V8 motor with a high (11.25:1) compression ratio and three Rochester two-barrel carburetors that GM referred to as 'Tri-power' induction. With this high performance engine, the El Camino's power and torque are outstanding.

Solid valve lifters

'Tri-power' induction

Cast-iron exhaust manifolds

Heavy cast-iron cylinder block

Cats-eye

Being the first of the line and having been built in the most glamorous era of American cars, the 1959 El Camino is the collector's dream. Big fins, 'cats-eye' taillamps and headlamp 'eyebrows' make it the most stylish of all luxury pick-up trucks.

The 1959 El Camino had all the stylish embellishments of the era.

Chevrolet **EL CAMINO**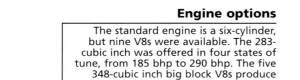

Stung by the success of the Ford Ranchero luxury sedan/pick-up, Chevrolet hit back with the El Camino. In its most powerful form, the El Camino was the fastest utility vehicle in the world.

Engine options
The standard engine is a six-cylinder, but nine V8s were available. The 283-cubic inch was offered in four states of tune, from 185 bhp to 290 bhp. The five 348-cubic inch big block V8s produce between 250 bhp and 315 bhp.

Limited slip differential
With the big block engines, traction off the line is poor. A Positraction limited slip differential was a sensible option at just $48.

Horizontal fins
One of the most distinctive features of all 1959 Chevrolets is the tailfin.

Luggage area in cab
You don't have to carry all your luggage in the cargo area; there is a small space behind the bench seat.

Air-conditioning
Despite the utilitarian interior, air-conditioning was available for $468.

Double-skinned bed
Although much of the El Camino is for show, Chevrolet made sure it was practical, too. The cargo area has a double-skinned load bed with a strong, ribbed-steel floor.

Live axle
Following typical Detroit fashion in the 1950s, the El Camino has a solid rear axle. Like Chevy wagons, the rear suspension has a Panhard rod and control arms to help to keep the axle in place. Rear coil springs help to smooth out the ride.

Twin headlights

Introduced on passenger cars in 1958, twin headlights remained a feature on the 1959 El Camino.

Wraparound windshield

Panoramic windshields were in fashion during the 1950s and offer excellent visibility.

Corvette transmission

Although a three-speed manual column shift was standard, the El Camino could be ordered with either an automatic or a floor-mounted Corvette four-speed transmission.

Specifications
1959 Chevrolet El Camino

ENGINE
Type: V8
Construction: Cast-iron block and heads
Valve gear: Two valves per cylinder operated by single central camshaft via pushrods, rockers and solid lifters
Bore and stroke: 4.13 in. x 3.27 in.
Displacement: 348 c.i.
Compression ratio: 11.25:1
Fuel system: Triple Rochester two-barrel carburetors
Maximum power: 315 bhp at 5,600 rpm
Maximum torque: 357 lb-ft at 3,600 rpm
Top speed: 131 mph
0–60 mph: 8.7 sec.

TRANSMISSION
Optional three-or four-speed manual or two-speed automatic

BODY/CHASSIS
Steel box section cruciform chassis with two-door pick-up body

SPECIAL FEATURES

The back of the roof projected outward and had the same 'flyaway' style feature as seen on 1959 Chevrolet hardtop sedans.

'Cats eye' tail-lights were a unique feature on Chevys of the period and were neatly split for the El Camino's tailgate.

RUNNING GEAR
Steering: Recirculating ball
Front suspension: Double wishbones with coil springs and telescopic shocks
Rear suspension: Live axle with trailing arms, Panhard rod and central torque reaction arm, coil springs and telescopic shocks
Brakes: Drums, 11-in. dia.
Wheels: Pressed steel, 14-in. dia.
Tires: Crossply 8.00 x 14

DIMENSIONS
Length: 210.9 in.
Width: 79.9 in.
Height: 58.7 in.
Wheelbase: 119.7 in.
Track: 60.2 in. (front), 59.5 in. (rear)
Weight: 3,881 lbs.

Chevrolet SUBURBAN

Launched in 1935, the Suburban is one of Chevy's best-loved and longest-lasting nameplates. With examples like this outstanding high-riding 1966 model, it is easy to see why.

"...a perfect match."

"If there was ever a near-perfect match between classic looks and modern levels of comfort and dependability, this is it. The seats are supportive and the cabin is light-years away from a stock 1966 Suburban. Performance is better, especially with a 300-bhp small-block under the hood. This rig can hold its own on the highway and gobbles up the miles with ease, but with its big, grippy tires and strong 4-WD driveline, it makes light work of rock crawling, too."

Digital gauges and modern seats are a tasteful and practical addition.

Milestones

1935 The Model EB Suburban, a steel-bodied station wagon built off the Master Series Truck, arrives on the scene. It can seat eight people and is offered with a number of different door configurations.

The shorter C/K-5™ Blazer™ supplemented the Suburban from 1969.

1960 Like the rest of Chevy's C10 series, the Suburban gets new angular sheetmetal, yet is still available with rear doors or a tailgate, plus six cylinder or V8 power.

Suburbans are still built off the full-size pickup platform.

1962 The full-size trucks revert to single headlamps and front-end styling, and model designations are simplified.

1966 A revamped C10 arrives.

UNDER THE SKIN

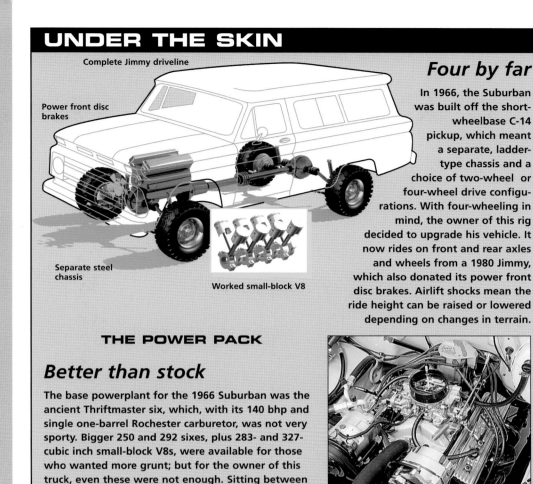

Complete Jimmy driveline

Power front disc brakes

Separate steel chassis

Worked small-block V8

Four by far

In 1966, the Suburban was built off the short-wheelbase C-14 pickup, which meant a separate, ladder-type chassis and a choice of two-wheel or four-wheel drive configurations. With four-wheeling in mind, the owner of this rig decided to upgrade his vehicle. It now rides on front and rear axles and wheels from a 1980 Jimmy, which also donated its power front disc brakes. Airlift shocks mean the ride height can be raised or lowered depending on changes in terrain.

THE POWER PACK

Better than stock

The base powerplant for the 1966 Suburban was the ancient Thriftmaster six, which, with its 140 bhp and single one-barrel Rochester carburetor, was not very sporty. Bigger 250 and 292 sixes, plus 283- and 327-cubic inch small-block V8s, were available for those who wanted more grunt; but for the owner of this truck, even these were not enough. Sitting between the light blue fenderwells is a 1970-vintage 350-cubic inch motor. With an 8.5:1 compression ratio, Edelbrock Performer intake manifold, and four-barrel carburetor, it packs a whopping 300 bhp and 380 lb-ft of torque.

Sixties simplicity

Back in the 1960s, the Suburban was far from the luxury wagon it is today. Most were still purchased for commercial duties, which explains why only 12,051 were built for 1966. Nevertheless, these old trucks possess plenty of character and simple, robust mechanicals, making them ideal candidates for resto-mod duty.

With only a few modifications, this 1966 Suburban really turns heads.

33

Chevrolet SUBURBAN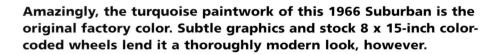

Amazingly, the turquoise paintwork of this 1966 Suburban is the original factory color. Subtle graphics and stock 8 x 15-inch color-coded wheels lend it a thoroughly modern look, however.

Final year styling

The 1966 full-size truck were the final iteration of the 1960 design. Ov the seasons, the appearance of these ri was cleaned up to satis buyer tastes. The grill and hood brightwork were simplified for 196 and single headlamps returned for the first time. The 1967 line wa even cleaner.

Jimmy suspension

With greater ground clearance than a stock K-14 Suburban, this vehicle owes its increased ride height to a 1980-vintage GMC Jimmy. The modern sport utility also donated its front and rear axles, plus the center differential. With less weight than a stock 1980 Jimmy, this Suburban can tackle all but the roughest terrain with considerable ease.

Rear tailgate

In 1966, as today, the Suburban could be ordered with either twin rear hinging doors or a drop-down tailgate. This one has the latter and it opens in two sections making the truck easier to load and unload.

Original and modern

One of the most appealing aspects of this truck is the interior. The stock dash is kept, but the instruments have been replaced. The old seats have been replaced by late-model buckets, which offer more support for the driver and passengers.

Hi-po small-block

A torquey 350-cubic inch V8 is just the ticket for towing and off-road excursions. With 380 lb-ft, it can power the Suburban to 60 mph in 10.4 seconds.

Specifications

1966 Chevrolet Suburban

ENGINE
Type: V8

Construction: Cast-iron block and heads

Valve gear: Two valves per cylinder operated by a single V-mounted camshaft with pushrods and rockers

Bore and stroke: 4.00 in. x 3.48 in.

Displacement: 350 c.i.

Compression ratio: 8.5:1

Induction system: Edelbrock Performer four-barrel carburetor

Maximum power: 300 bhp at 4,800 rpm

Maximum torque: 380 lb-ft at 3,200 rpm

Top speed: 114 mph

0–60 mph: 10.4 sec.

TRANSMISSION
700RS four-speed automatic

BODY/CHASSIS
Separate steel chassis with two-door station wagon body

SPECIAL FEATURES

The embroidered bowtie logo on the headrest is just one of several subtle touches.

These wheels are stock items on 1980 Blazers and Jimmys.

RUNNING GEAR
Steering: Recirculating-ball

Front suspension: Live axle with semi-elliptic leaf springs and telescopic shock absorbers

Rear suspension: Live axle with semi-elliptic leaf springs and telescopic shock absorbers

Brakes: Discs (front), drums (rear)

Wheels: Pressed steel, 8 x 15 in.

Tires: BF Goodrich All Terrain

DIMENSIONS
Length: 193.19 in. **Width:** 86.8 in.

Height: 81.6 in. **Wheelbase:** 115.0 in.

Track: 74.9 in. (front), 66.7 in. (rear)

Weight: 3,850 lbs.

Chevrolet BLAZER K5

The K10 Blazer is big, tough and rugged, and the immortal Chevy® V8 gives it the power to go anywhere. Since its revision in the 1990s, the Blazer is more civilized than the traditional Jeep.

1979

"...four-wheel traction."

"On open roads, the full-size Blazer cruises effortlessly at around 70 mph, but its total lack of aerodynamics blunts performance above that speed. It has a harsh, choppy ride on poor surfaces due to its stiff leaf springs, but on a smooth road the big Blazer can hustle around corners. Off-road, and with low range selected, it will charge its way up, over or through just about anything. Even now, the Blazer is a great off-roader."

The utilitarian interior of the Blazer suits the requirements of the off-road driver.

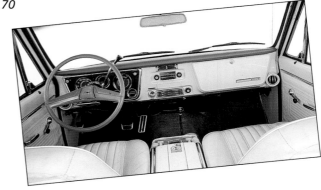

Milestones

1969 Chevrolet introduces
the Blazer as a roomy two- or four-wheel drive utility vehicle for use both on and off road. The base engine is a 120-bhp, 250-cubic inch straight-six, but Chevrolet's small-block 307 and 350 V8s are also available.

The first generation Blazers were crude, but tough.

1973 To bring it
up to date. the Blazer receives a major facelift, including a larger, less boxy body. This style remains, albeit with minor detail changes, until well into the 1980s.

The 1998 Blazer is in fact an S10 and uses a V6 engine.

1992 A revised Blazer,
with independent wishbone front suspension, a five-speed transmission and anti-lock brakes is introduced. This version is bigger than the first Blazer and has a longer wheelbase.

UNDER THE SKIN

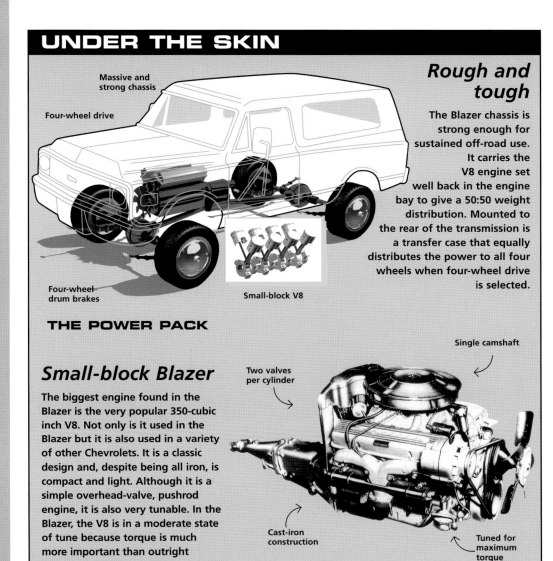

Massive and strong chassis

Four-wheel drive

Four-wheel drum brakes

Small-block V8

Rough and tough

The Blazer chassis is strong enough for sustained off-road use. It carries the V8 engine set well back in the engine bay to give a 50:50 weight distribution. Mounted to the rear of the transmission is a transfer case that equally distributes the power to all four wheels when four-wheel drive is selected.

THE POWER PACK

Small-block Blazer

The biggest engine found in the Blazer is the very popular 350-cubic inch V8. Not only is it used in the Blazer but it is also used in a variety of other Chevrolets. It is a classic design and, despite being all iron, is compact and light. Although it is a simple overhead-valve, pushrod engine, it is also very tunable. In the Blazer, the V8 is in a moderate state of tune because torque is much more important than outright power.

Two valves per cylinder

Single camshaft

Cast-iron construction

Tuned for maximum torque

Still going

The full-size Blazer has survived into the 1990s even though it has been supplemented by the popular, but smaller, S10. It has become more advanced, with the introduction of independent front suspension and a five-speed manual transmission. The S10 is now known as the Blazer and the full-size truck is called the Tahoe®.

The smaller S10® Blazer arrived in 1983. This is a 1993 model.

Chevrolet **BLAZER K5**

The early model Blazer is not glamorous, but that's the last thing on your mind when you're miles from civilization. In these conditions you appreciate the truck's good qualities—simplicity, strength and reliability.

Permanent four-wheel drive

Drive to all four wheels is permanently engaged, with the torque split equally front and rear.

Limited slip differential

For even more traction, limited slip differentials can be added to the axles, but they are not standard equipment.

V8 engine

The 350-cubic inch small-block V8 which powers many other popular Chevrolets is equally capable in the off-road K5; but here it's tuned for torque, not power.

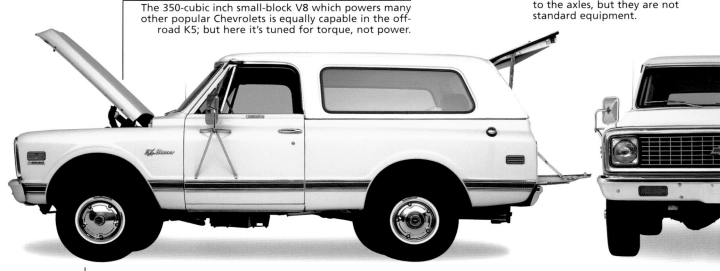

Front disc brakes

Most of the braking is undertaken by the front wheels, and so the Blazer has optional front discs. Drum brakes are retained at the rear.

Rear tailgate

The rear tailgate folds flat, level with the floor, to allow loads to be slid inside. To carry large items, however, the spare wheel has to be removed.

Live axles

Blazers are traditional off-road vehicles, with live axles at both the front and rear supported by semi-elliptic leaf springs. This system is extremely strong and allows excellent axle articulation in off-road conditions.

High and low ratio

For road driving, the normal high range of gears is used, but for difficult off-road conditions and climbing, the Blazer has a lower ratio to take better advantage of its torque.

High ground clearance

The body sits 8.5 inches off the ground to avoid damage from tree stumps and small rocks when four-wheeling. The clearance between the wheel and the body gives room for extreme suspension travel.

Specifications

1969 Chevrolet Blazer K5

ENGINE

Type: V8

Construction: Cast-iron block and cylinder heads

Valve gear: Two valves per cylinder operated by a single block-mounted camshaft, pushrods, rockers and hydraulic lifters

Bore and stroke: 4 in. x 3.48 in.

Displacement: 350 c.i.

Compression ratio: 8.5:1

Induction system: Single four-barrel Rochester carburetor

Maximum power: 165 bhp at 3,800 rpm

Maximum torque: 255 lb-ft at 2,800 rpm

Top speed: 98 mph

0–60 mph: 15.0 sec.

TRANSMISSION

Three-speed Turbo HydraMatic automatic, with two-speed transfer case and high and low ratios

BODY/CHASSIS

Separate chassis with steel five-door utility body

SPECIAL FEATURES

Large door mirrors are optional and allow a larger rear view when towing.

Front disc brakes are a worthwhile option for improved braking.

RUNNING GEAR

Steering: Recirculating ball

Front suspension: Live axle with semi-elliptic leaf springs and telescopic shock absorbers

Rear suspension: Live axle with semi-elliptic leaf springs and telescopic shock absorbers

Brakes: Discs, 11.6 in. dia. (front), drums, 11.1 in. dia. (rear)

Wheels: Pressed steel, 6 in. x 15 in.

Tires: LT10.15 H78 x 15

DIMENSIONS

Length: 184.4 in.   **Width:** 79.6 in.

Height: 73.1 in.   **Wheelbase:** 106.5 in.

Track: 66.7 in. (front), 63.7 in. (rear)

Weight: 5,157 lbs.

Chevrolet **EL CAMINO SS454**

Part car, part truck—the El Camino was always an exclusive vehicle. In the late 1960s, however, the horsepower race could not be ignored, and in 1970 Chevrolet released the meanest El Camino of them all—the SS454.

"...Super Sport hauler."

"From behind the wheel you would think you were sitting in a Chevelle™ SS™: the dashboard, front bucket seats and console are identical. It feels the same too, with a throaty growl from the big V8 and instant acceleration. However, with an unloaded bed, great care is needed when cornering and braking because it's easy to bring out the rear end. At the drag strip this particular El Camino is unique—few pick ups are capable of 14-second ¼-mile times."

Sportiness abounds inside, with front bucket seats and full instrumentation.

Milestones

1964 After a four-year

absence the El Camino is relaunched, although it is now based on the midsize Chevelle. A Super Sport package is available, and a big-block 396-cubic inch V8 is optional from 1966.

In 1959, the El Camino was revealed as a stylish pick up.

1968 This year the

El Camino receives a major facelift with softer, more flowing styling. Engines range from a straight-six to the 396-cubic inch V8.

1970 Like the Chevelle SS, the El

Camino is now available with a 454-cubic inch V8 in either 360-bhp or 450-bhp tune.

In 1970, the Chevelle SS rode the same chassis as the El Camino.

1971 The El Camino

SS454 returns, but the 450-bhp LS6 engine is dropped and all V8s have lowered compression; performance and horsepower are also down. A restyled El Camino is still available with the 454-cubic inch V8.

UNDER THE SKIN

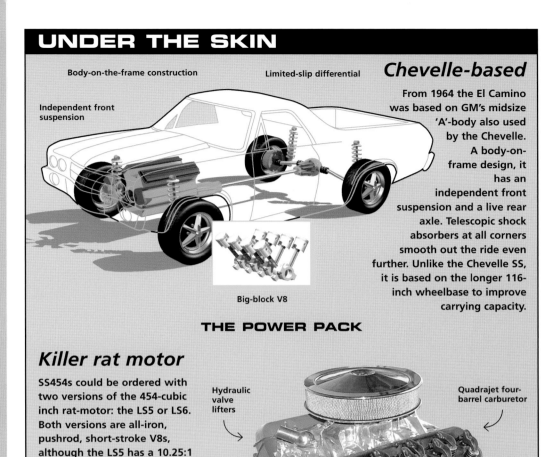

Body-on-the-frame construction

Limited-slip differential

Independent front suspension

Big-block V8

Chevelle-based

From 1964 the El Camino was based on GM's midsize 'A'-body also used by the Chevelle. A body-on-frame design, it has an independent front suspension and a live rear axle. Telescopic shock absorbers at all corners smooth out the ride even further. Unlike the Chevelle SS, it is based on the longer 116-inch wheelbase to improve carrying capacity.

THE POWER PACK

Killer rat motor

SS454s could be ordered with two versions of the 454-cubic inch rat-motor: the LS5 or LS6. Both versions are all-iron, pushrod, short-stroke V8s, although the LS5 has a 10.25:1 compression ratio, hydraulic valve lifters and is rated at 360 bhp. The LS6 features forged-aluminum pistons and forged-steel crankshaft and connection rods. Topped by a huge Holley 850-cfm four-barrel carburetor, it puts out an incredible 450 bhp and 500 lb-ft of torque.

Hydraulic valve lifters

Quadrajet four-barrel carburetor

Cast-iron block and cylinder heads

Forged-steel crankshaft

Power lust

The most desirable of all El Caminos is the 1970 SS454 equipped with the LS6 engine. This monster thumps out 450 bhp and is the quickest of all El Caminos. Only a handful were built and they are now highly sought-after for their performance.

The 1970 LS6-engined El Camino SS454 was only built for one year.

Chevrolet **EL CAMINO SS454**

The SS454 was the pinnacle of the El Camino's career. It has the perfect combination of style and practicality, together with the sheer power and performance of the big-block V8.

Disc brakes

Early El Camino SS models could definitely go, but stopping was more of a problem. By 1970 the Super Sport package offered power front disc brakes, which helped make the monster pickup slightly safer.

Big-block V8

The Turbo Jet 454 engine was available in two states of tune. The hydraulic lifter LS5 (as fitted to this car) was rated at 360 bhp and the killer LS-6 at 450 bhp.

Bench or buckets

Like the Chevelle, the El Camino could be specified with either a front bench or twin bucket seats. This example has bucket seats with a center-mounted console. The dashboard layout on both models is identical.

Large load area

The El Camino was extremely practical with a load area of 32.14 sq ft.

Positraction differential

The combination of an empty load bed and 500 lb-ft of torque can result in the rear wheels spinning under hard acceleration. An optional Positraction limited-slip differential helps to reduce this.

Close-ratio four-speed

To handle all the torque from the Turbojet LS5 engine, this El Camino uses a Muncie M21 close-ratio four-speed transmission. It is named after GM's transmission plant in Muncie, Indiana.

Dealer-installed tarp

To help protect both the bed and loads, a dealer-installed tarp was available.

Specifications

1970 Chevrolet El Camino SS454

ENGINE

Type: V8

Construction: Cast-iron block and heads

Valve gear: Two valves per cylinder operated by a single camshaft via pushrods, rockers and hydraulic lifters

Bore and stroke: 4.25 in. x 4.00 in.

Displacement: 454 c.i.

Compression ratio: 10.25:1

Induction system: Single Rochester Quadrajet four-barrel carburetor

Maximum power: 360 bhp at 4,400 rpm

Maximum torque: 500 lb-ft at 3,200 rpm

Top speed: 130 mph

0–60 mph: 7.0 sec.

TRANSMISSION

Muncie M21 (close ratio) four-speed

BODY/CHASSIS

Separate steel perimeter frame with two-door cabin and exposed cargo area

SPECIAL FEATURES

For 1970 only, El Camino SS models were fitted with these Magnum 500 Super Sport wheels.

A special cowl induction hood draws air into the engine at the base of the windshield.

RUNNING GEAR

Steering: Recirculating ball

Front suspension: Double wishbones with coil springs, telescopic shock absorbers and anti-roll bar

Rear suspension: Live axle with control arms, coil springs and telescopic shock absorbers

Brakes: Discs, 11.0-in. dia (front), drums, 9.5-in. dia (rear)

Wheels: Magnum 500, 7 x 15 in.

Tires: HR70-15

DIMENSIONS

Length: 206.8 in.   **Width:** 75.4 in.

Height: 54.4 in.   **Wheelbase:** 116.0 in.

Track: 60.2 in. (front), 59.2 in. (rear)

Weight: 4,270 lbs.

Chevrolet S10 PICKUP

A domestic response to the number of minitrucks imported into the U.S. during the early 1980s, the S10 soon became a best-seller and a favorite with the aftermarket crowd.

"...modified mini hauler."

"It may be small and boxy, but the S10 is a favorite custom ride and after spending time driving it you begin to see why. The Vortech V6 is a real stump-puller at low revs and the 700R4 transmission really enables you to get the best from it. Riding on a lowered suspension means that the ride can get a little bumpy over less-than-ideal road surfaces, but in terms of handling, this modified mini hauler corners with the best of the factory hot-rod pickups."

Front seats from a Plymouth Laser offer greater support than the stock buckets.

Milestones

1982 Chevrolet
replaces the LUV, its import, with the S10, a new pickup. It comes with a 1.9 cylinder engine, though a 2.8-liter V6 is optional.

The Syclone™ and Typhoon™ versions of the S10/Sonoma™ family are the most popular among buyers.

1983 An extended-cab model, four-wheel
drive and a 2.0-liter four are new this year. A companion S10 Blazer SUV also debuts.

The current S10 still uses the same chassis and engine.

1985 Trim is revised
and 4x4 models get a standard 2.5-liter fuel injected engine.

1988 A bigger
4.3-liter V6 power plant becomes available.

1993 Production
is brought to an end.

UNDER THE SKIN

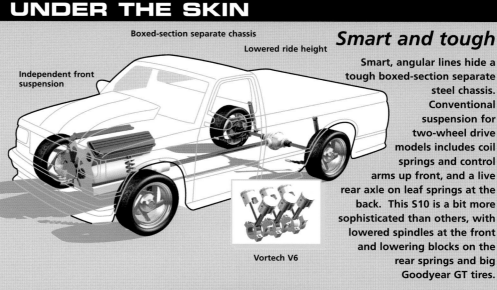

Boxed-section separate chassis

Lowered ride height

Independent front suspension

Vortech V6

Smart and tough

Smart, angular lines hide a tough boxed-section separate steel chassis. Conventional suspension for two-wheel drive models includes coil springs and control arms up front, and a live rear axle on leaf springs at the back. This S10 is a bit more sophisticated than others, with lowered spindles at the front and lowering blocks on the rear springs and big Goodyear GT tires.

THE POWER PACK

Viva Vortech

The biggest engine available in the 1984 S10 was a sluggish 173-cubic inch (2.8-liter) V6. This owner replaced the original motor with something more powerful: the 4.3 liter Vortech V6, which offers more power. The 1990 4.3-liter Vortech V6 that now sits between the fenders offers considerably more grunt. Adapted from the Chevy™ V-8 it is fairly low-tech, with a cast-iron block and cylinder heads, plus two valves per cylinder actuated by pushrods and hydraulic lifters with a block-mounted camshaft. With throttle-body electronic fuel injection, it cranks out 160 bhp and 230 lb-ft of torque.

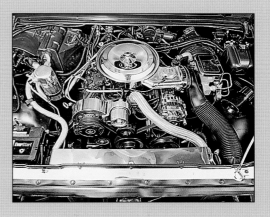

Steady S10

The S10 was among the first wave of true domestic compact pickups. Remaining in production for over a decade, it was improved, with powerful engines, more comfort and greater capability. It is also relatively easy to modify.

Original S10s have a heavy-duty look that attracts customizers.

Chevrolet S10 PICKUP

At a glance, it may look more or less like a standard S10 with aftermarket wheels, but this truck is full of clever and subtle touches that makes it stand out everywhere it goes.

Vortech V6 engine

Replacing the fairly anemic 2.8-liter V6 is a 4.3-liter Vortech unit. This was the most powerful engine offered in a compact pickup in 1989-1990. It was also used in later models of the S10 and Blazer.

Custom-made rear bumpers

Although most of the body panel extensions are from the Stillen parts catalog, the rear bumpers are custom-fabricated items. They blend in well with the other extension pieces.

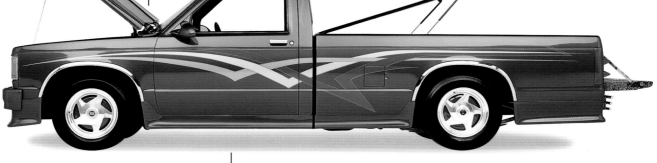

Lowered suspension

One of the first modifications carried out on a minitruck was to drop the suspension. The desired effect has been achieved on this truck by lowering spindles (at the front) and lowering blocks (on the rear leaf springs).

Color-coded interior

Replacing the stock seats are more supportive Plymouth Laser buckets. These have been upholstered in teal green fabric, which is color-matched to the rest of the interior.

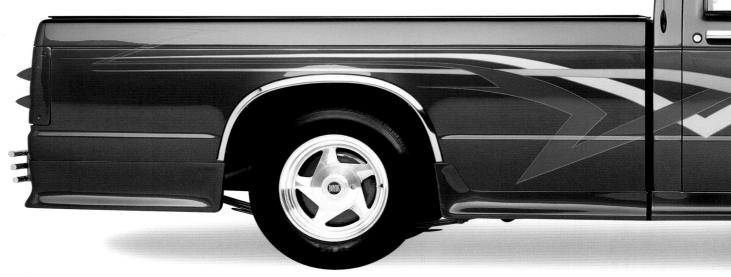

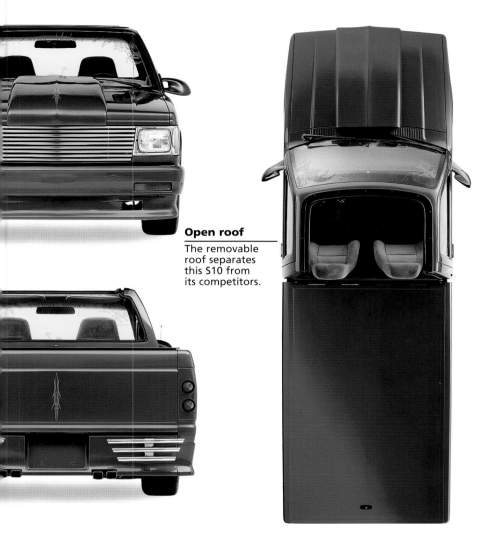

Open roof

The removable roof separates this S10 from its competitors.

Cowl-induction hood scoop

Functional hood scoops draw air away from the windshield pressure area and into the engine compartments; they also vent hot underhood air at low speeds.

Specifications

1984 Chevrolet S10

ENGINE

Type: V6

Construction: Cast-iron block and heads

Valve gear: Two valves per cylinder operated by a single V-mounted camshaft with pushrods and rockers

Bore and stroke: 4.00 in. x 3.48 in.

Displacement: 4.3 liter

Compression ratio: 8.6:1

Induction system: Throttle-body fuel injection

Maximum power: 160 bhp at 4,000 rpm

Maximum torque: 230 lb-ft at 2,800 rpm

Top speed: 108 mph

0–60 mph: 11.2 sec.

TRANSMISSION

GM 700R-4 four-speed automatic

BODY/CHASSIS

Separate steel chassis with two-door steel cab

SPECIAL FEATURES

Customizing on the differential carrier extends the personal touch on this S10.

The removable roof adds a bit of novelty to this S10.

RUNNING GEAR

Steering: Recirculating-ball

Front suspension: Unequal-length A-arms, coil springs, telescopic shock absorbers and anti-roll bar

Rear suspension: Live axle, semi elliptic leaf springs and telescopic shock absorbers

Brakes: Discs (front), drums (rear)

Wheels: Boyd Billet aluminum 15 x 7 in. (front), 15x 8 in. (rear)

Tires: Goodyear radial

DIMENSIONS

Length: 177.5 in. **Width:** 64.8 in.

Height: 52.3 in.   **Wheelbase:** 108.3 in.

Track: 49.0 (front), 49.5 (rear)

Weight: 3,140 lbs.

Chevrolet 454 SS

As performance made a comeback in the late 1980s, a new automotive phenomenon began to take hold in the U.S.—muscle trucks. One of the first to arrive on the scene was the potent Chevrolet 454 SS.

"...massive amount of torque."

"When you take your place behind the wheel, the 454 feels almost like any other C/K-series pickup. The coil-sprung front suspension gives the SS a smoother ride than most trucks of the era, but the lightly loaded back end can get upset over rough surfaces. What really sets this truck apart, however, is its massive amount of torque. With a large engine, acceleration from the lights is tremendous and it pulls the full-size pickup all the way to 120 mph."

Dual bucket seats are comfortable and give the big truck a dash of sportiness.

Milestones

1988 Chevrolet releases a radically reworked version of its popular full-size pickup. It boasts up-to-the-minute styling, an improved interior, a stiffer frame and better handling and ride.

The huge Suburban™ shares its sheet metal with the C1500.

1989 Realizing that there is a potential market for performance pickups, Chevrolet decides to drop its monster 454 engine into the standard-cab, short-bed C1500 truck. The resulting 454 SS goes on sale as a 1990 model. It is initially available only in black.

Chevy 2500 pickups could be offered with a 454-cubic inch V8 but in lower tune than the SS.

1992 There are few changes for the 454 SS, but the color choice is expanded to include red and white.

1993 Having spawned a number of competitors, production of the 454 SS comes to an end.

UNDER THE SKIN

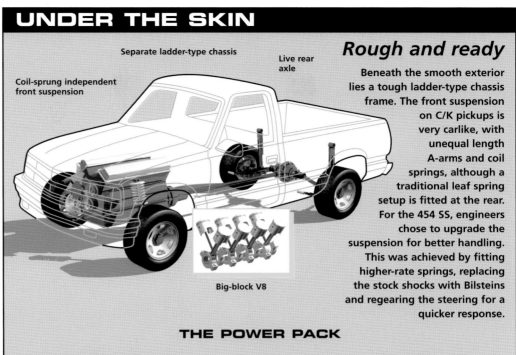

Separate ladder-type chassis

Live rear axle

Coil-sprung independent front suspension

Big-block V8

Rough and ready

Beneath the smooth exterior lies a tough ladder-type chassis frame. The front suspension on C/K pickups is very carlike, with unequal length A-arms and coil springs, although a traditional leaf spring setup is fitted at the rear. For the 454 SS, engineers chose to upgrade the suspension for better handling. This was achieved by fitting higher-rate springs, replacing the stock shocks with Bilsteins and regearing the steering for a quicker response.

THE POWER PACK

Gen V big block

Chevrolet was first on the scene with a muscle truck, and for maximum impact it decided to fit the largest engine it could. The huge 454-cubic-inch engine, used in the standard C/K 3/4- and 1-ton pickups, was chosen. With a fairly long stroke, it is designed for power and torque delivery at low rpm, making it extremely tractable under normal driving conditions. Updates to the 454 unit in the SS truck included Delco electronic ignition, low restriction cast-iron exhaust manifolds and a new intake.

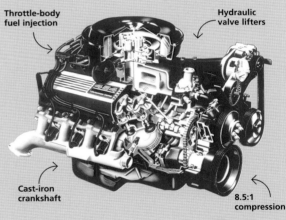

Throttle-body fuel injection

Hydraulic valve lifters

Cast-iron crankshaft

8.5:1 compression

Collector C/K

Among the 1988-1998 generation of C/K-series trucks, the 454 SS is the most sought after. It boasts more power than the others and has truly phenomenal acceleration, improved handling and unique paint and graphics. Good ones can sell for $12,000.

Among all C/K-series trucks, the 1991 454 SS is the best performer.

Chevrolet 454 SS

With this high performance truck, Chevrolet uncovered a new market for factory hot rodded pickups. When the 454 SS first appeared, the division could claim that it was the most powerful production pickup truck on sale at the time.

Smooth styling

Smoother, more rounded styling marked a dramatic departure from the rough-and-ready look of previous Chevy trucks. Until 1992, these aero-styled trucks were available only in standard cab form.

Stiffened frame

When the new big pickups arrived for 1988, Chevrolet engineers paid considerable attention to the chassis, strengthening the crossmembers and adding thicker rubber bushings to increase stiffness.

Front disc brakes

By the 1990s, many full-size trucks had front disc brakes. The SS is no exception, although 9.5-inch drums are still fitted at the rear. Anti-lock braking (ABS) is standard.

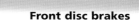

Rugged rear end

In 1990, a TH400 three-speed was coupled to a 10-bolt differential with 3.73:1 gears. In 1991, an all new 4L80-E four-speed automatic was introduced. It was basically an electronically shifted TH400, but with overdrive. In addition to the new transmission, the truck also came with steeper 4.10:1 gears.

Handling suspension

Because buyers wanted muscle trucks to go around corners as well as they could accelerate in a straight line, the 454 SS was treated to suspension upgrades. The ZQ6 setup, with stiffer front coil and rear leaf springs, was specified, as were Bilstein shocks and a beefy front anti-roll bar. This results in the truck having a street-rod-like raked stance.

Monster powerplant

Chevrolet's catch phrase in the early 1990s was 'The Heartbeat of America.' The heartbeat of this truck is one of the largest engines ever shoehorned into a production pickup. With 405 lb-ft of torque under the hood, it was a serious street brawler.

Less restrictive exhaust system

In 1991, GM replaced the truck's single exhaust with a true dual system. The change brought power up to 255 bhp and 405 lb-ft of torque. This figure is up from 230 bhp and 385 lb-ft of torque in 1990.

Specifications

1991 Chevrolet 454 SS

ENGINE

Type: V8

Construction: Cast-iron block and heads

Valve gear: Two valves per cylinder operated by a single camshaft with pushrods and rockers

Bore and stroke: 4.25 in. x 4.00 in.

Displacement: 454 c.i.

Compression ratio: 8.5: 1

Induction system: Throttle-body fuel injection

Maximum power: 255 bhp at 4,000 rpm

Maximum torque: 405 lb-ft at 2,400 rpm

Top speed: 120 mph

0–60 mph: 7.2 sec.

TRANSMISSION

GM 700R4 three-speed automatic

BODY/CHASSIS

Steel ladder frame with steel cab and bed

SPECIAL FEATURES

In the SS, the 7.4-liter big-block engine was known as the Tonawanda V8.

These slotted aluminum wheels are unique to Chevrolet 454 SS pickups.

RUNNING GEAR

Steering: Recirculating ball

Front suspension: Unequal-length A-arms with coil springs, telescopic shock absorbers and anti-roll bar

Rear suspension: Live axle with semi-elliptic leaf springs, coil springs and telescopic shock absorbers

Brakes: Discs (front), drums (rear)

Wheels: Cast-aluminum, 15-in. dia.

Tires: Goodyear GT+4, P225/60 VR15

DIMENSIONS

Length: 185.1 in. **Width:** 75.4 in.

Height: 77.9 in. **Wheelbase:** 115.0 in.

Track: 62.8 in. (front), 61.9 in. (rear)

Weight: 4,535 lbs.

Dodge A100

A rival to the Ford Econoline and Chevy Greenbriar, the Dodge A100 was a no-frills, light-duty delivery truck. However, with a little ingenuity it could be transformed into a hot little street pickup.

"...substantial torque."

"When describing the A100, small and spartan are the words that come to mind. A three-speed manual transmission and skinny steering wheel remind you how different vehicles of the 1960s were. Turn the key and the first surprise awaits you. Instead of a plodding six under the floorboards, there's a 273 small-block V8. With substantial torque on tap, three speeds is all you need. Low weight means wheelspin can be a problem, but also enables this truck to accelerate quickly."

Although it features a CD player and custom seats, the cab still has an aura of functionality.

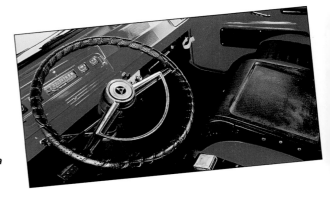

Milestones

1964 February sees the arrival of the A100 series. It is available as a pickup, panel van or Sportsman wagon. Powering the A100s is a 170-cubic inch slant-six engine and three-speed manual transmission. Drag racer Bill 'Maverick' Golden stuffs a 426 Hemi into an A100 and hits the strips. His rig, called the 'Little Red Wagon,' becomes known for its wheelstanding antics.

Ford's original Econoline was a rival to the A100.

1967 A long-wheelbase van and

Sportsman, offering 43 cubic feet more interior space, join the lineup. The optional V8 is bored out from 273 to 318 cubic inches.

The current Dakota is far removed from the A100.

1970 In its final year, the A100 series

gets a fully synchronized manual transmission and a bigger 198-cubic inch six as the base engine.

UNDER THE SKIN

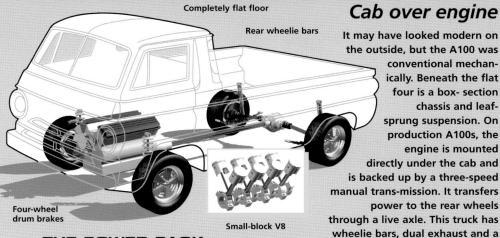

Completely flat floor

Rear wheelie bars

Four-wheel drum brakes

Small-block V8

Cab over engine

It may have looked modern on the outside, but the A100 was conventional mechanically. Beneath the flat four is a box-section chassis and leaf-sprung suspension. On production A100s, the engine is mounted directly under the cab and is backed up by a three-speed manual trans-mission. It transfers power to the rear wheels through a live axle. This truck has wheelie bars, dual exhaust and a set of 3.91:1 rear gears.

THE POWER PACK

Free-revving V8

Chrysler's near-bulletproof 170-cubic inch slant six was standard in A100s, but a larger 225 version was available for those who wanted greater torque. 1965, its second year in production, saw the intro-duction of a 273-cubic inch V8 on the option list. It enabled Dodge to introduce the first compact truck available with V8 power. The V8 in this A100 is the 273-cubic inch mill that was offered in 1965. The cast-iron small-block unit, even in two-barrel form, is a rev-happy unit with a smooth power delivery, qualities that endear it to hot-rodders. Adding a four-barrel carburetor and 10.5:1-compression pistons resulted in a pavement-pounding 235 bhp.

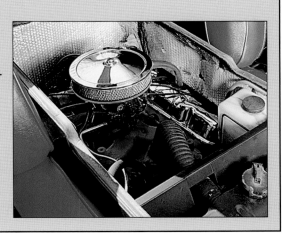

Wheelstander

Built in sizable numbers between 1964 and 1970, the A100 is not exactly a collectible commodity. Even the V8 versions, while consid-erably rarer than the sixes, can be bought for around $3,000 in excellent condition and make a great starting point for a trick street hauler. One A100 that does stand above the rest is the 'Little Red Wagon' drag race truck.

This truck has been styled like the famous 'Little Red Wagon.'

Dodge **A100** 🇺🇸

Bill Golden elevated the A100 to icon status with his 'Little Red Wagon' and inspired others to build their own versions. This rolling tribute combines the look of a 1960s custom hauler with modern comfort.

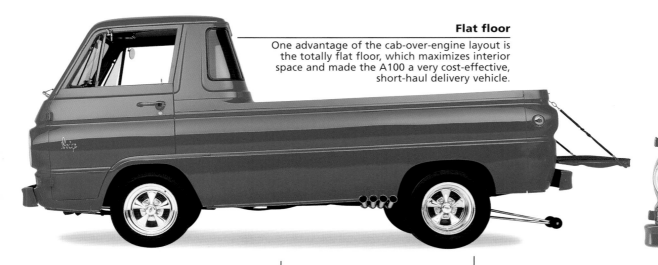

Flat floor

One advantage of the cab-over-engine layout is the totally flat floor, which maximizes interior space and made the A100 a very cost-effective, short-haul delivery vehicle.

Three-speed transmission

All A100s came standard with a three-speed manual transmission. However, buyers could order a three-speed Loadflite automatic, which came with a dash-mounted lever.

Classic Cragar wheels

In the 1960s, Cragar S/S wheels were very popular. In keeping with its vintage appearance, the rear wheels are five inches wider than those at the front giving it a real pro street look.

Updated interior

Intended primarily for work use, A100s had stripped out interiors. Because this truck is primarily for recreational purposes, the cabin has been fitted with a modern Sony CD stereo system, a custom-built overhead console and red and black leather seats.

Drum brakes

Very few vehicles had disc brakes in the mid-1960s, and all A100s came with standard four-wheel drum brakes. This truck retains the stock braking system.

ENGINE

Type: V8

Construction: Cast-iron block and heads

Valve gear: Two valves per cylinder operated by a single block-mounted camshaft with pushrods and rockers

Bore and stroke: 3.63 in. x 3.31 in.

Displacement: 273 c.i.

Compression ratio: 10.5:1

Induction system: Carter AFB four-barrel carburetor

Maximum power: 235 bhp at 5,200 rpm

Maximum torque: 280 lb-ft at 4,000 rpm

Top speed: 115 mph

0–60 mph: 8.4 sec.

TRANSMISSION

Three-speed manual

BODY/CHASSIS

Separate steel chassis with steel cab-over-engine pickup body

SPECIAL FEATURES

The wheelie bars on this truck are purely for looks and have no functional purpose.

Quad exhaust tips are similar to those found on 1960s drag racers.

RUNNING GEAR

Steering: Recirculating ball

Front suspension: Beam axle with semi-elliptic leaf springs and telescopic shock absorbers

Rear suspension: Live axle with semi-elliptic leaf springs and telescopic shock absorbers

Brakes: Drums (front and rear)

Wheels: Cragar S/S, 5 x 15 in. (front), 10 x 15 in. (rear)

Tires: BFGoodrich, 195/70 R15 (front), 295/50 R15 (rear)

DIMENSIONS

Length: 161.3 in.   **Width:** 75.9 in.

Height: 73.8 in.   **Wheelbase:** 90.0 in

Track: 58.6 in. (front), 55.7 in. (rear)

Weight: 3,010 lbs.

Dodge **RAM**

Since its introduction, the latest Ram, with its bold, extroverted styling, spacious interior, and unprecedented refinement, has proven immensely popular. It currently holds 12 percent of the full-size truck market.

"...rugged and spacious."

"From any angle the Ram is huge. Inside, it boasts one of the most spacious cabs in its class, with ample room even in standard form. Turning the key brings the huge V10 to life. The largest engine available in a production pick-up, it offers an incredible amount of power and torque. The column-shifted four-speed automatic is effortless. Rugged and spacious, the Dodge Ram is perfect for a night on the town or working on the ranch."

Inside, the Ram is car-like and boasts considerable refinement for a full-size pick-up.

Milestones

1994 After years of fielding
a boxy and outmoded design, Dodge jumps back into the truck market with a huge splash. The new Ram has bold styling and the best interior in its class.

Introduced in late 1997, the Quadcab has twin rear doors.

1995 In order to compete
with rival Ford, a Ram Sport model, with a body-colored grill and bumpers, is launched. It is only available in standard cab, short wheel-base configuration and a V8 is the only engine choice.

Big Ram styling cues have also been extended to the mid-size Dakota pick up, and the Durango sport utility (above).

1997 Turning the industry
on its ear yet again, Dodge introduces its unique Quadcab model, with suicide doors on both sides.

UNDER THE SKIN

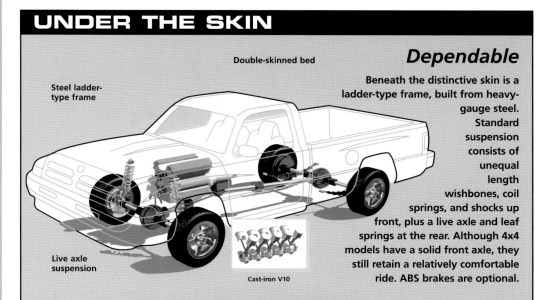

Double-skinned bed

Steel ladder-type frame

Live axle suspension

Cast-iron V10

Dependable

Beneath the distinctive skin is a ladder-type frame, built from heavy-gauge steel. Standard suspension consists of unequal length wishbones, coil springs, and shocks up front, plus a live axle and leaf springs at the rear. Although 4x4 models have a solid front axle, they still retain a relatively comfortable ride. ABS brakes are optional.

THE POWER PACK

Biggest ever

The current Ram is offered with a variety of engines, including a 3.9-liter (237 cubic inch) V6, two V8s and a diesel. Top of the range, available in ¾- and 1-ton models, is an 8.0-liter (488 cubic inch) V10, which is also used in the Dodge Viper. It retains two valves per cylinder and pushrods, but also incorporates a highly sophisticated sequential electronic fuel injection system. In the Ram, the V10 produces 300 bhp and a huge 440 lb-ft of torque at only 2,800 rpm. Despite this power, compression is relatively low at 8.6:1.

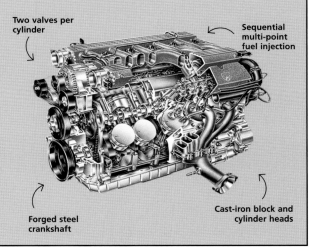

Two valves per cylinder

Sequential multi-point fuel injection

Forged steel crankshaft

Cast-iron block and cylinder heads

Macho style

Part of the Ram's tremendous sales appeal is its big grill and 18-wheeler appearance. This gives it a traditional all-American look combined with modern styling cues. Love it or hate it, you certainly cannot ignore the current Dodge Ram pickup.

With 440 lb-ft of torque the Ram is a great tow vehicle.

Dodge **RAM**

With the current Ram, Dodge is on to a winner. Buyers love the brawny exterior styling and the spacious and luxurious interior. A variety of body styles, lengths and powertrains is available.

Monster V10

The Ram is unique in being the only current American pickup to be fitted with a V10. Based on the Viper's engine, the truck unit is cast-iron instead of alloy but still produces an impressive 300 bhp.

Roll bar

Many 4x4 pick-ups are fitted with roll bars. Although they are installed for safety reasons, they also give the truck a rugged and durable look.

Car-like interior

Trevor Creed styled the interior and placed considerable emphasis on ergonomics with all controls logically placed. King-size cup holders are also fitted.

Different bed lengths

Like its main rivals, the Ram is available with two different bed lengths—6.5 and 8 feet. This example has the longer bed and is able to carry ¾-ton loads, as specified by its 2500 designation.

Optional ABS

With safety in mind, anti-lock brakes (ABS) are available and help stop rear-wheel lock-up with an empty load bed.

Big rig style

From the front, the Ram looks like a scaled-down Peterbilt or Freightliner conventional. This contrasts with the car-like appearance of other pickups.

Plush ride

With gas-filled shock absorbers, even 4x4 models, such as this 2500, offer a supple ride and make them ideal for regular open road use.

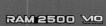

Specifications
1995 Dodge Ram 2500 V10

ENGINE
Type: V10
Construction: Cast-iron block and heads
Valve gear: Two valves per cylinder operated by pushrods and hydraulic lifters
Bore and stroke: 4 in. x 3.88 in.
Displacement: 488 c.i.
Compression ratio: 8.6:1
Induction system: Sequential multi-point fuel injection
Maximum power: 300 bhp at 4,000 rpm
Maximum torque: 440 lb-ft at 2,800 rpm
Top speed: 113 mph
0–60 mph: 7.5 sec

TRANSMISSION
Four-speed automatic

BODY/CHASSIS
Steel frame with separate steel body

SPECIAL FEATURES

Roll bar-mounted spotlights are a favorite accessory for many buyers.

Big Goodyear Wrangler off-road tires ensure maximum grip.

RUNNING GEAR
Steering: Recirculating ball
Front suspension: Live front axle with coil springs and telescopic shocks
Rear suspension: Live rear axle with multi-leaf springs and telescopic shocks
Brakes: Vented discs, 12.5-in. dia. (front), drums, 13-in. dia. (rear), optional ABS
Wheels: Styled steel, 16-in. dia.
Tires: Goodyear Wrangler RT/S P245/75R16

DIMENSIONS
Length: 224.3 in.   **Width:** 79.4 in.
Height: 72.1 in.   **Wheelbase:** 134.7 in.
Track: 68.6 in. (front), 68 in. (rear)
Weight: 5,383 lbs.

Dodge **DURANGO**

Unashamedly based on the Dakota truck, the new Dodge Durango SUV combines the best of both worlds: trucklike strength and size, and carlike comfort, ride and handling.

"...balanced and comfortable."

"For all its Dakota truck underpinnings the Durango does everything many more purpose-built SUVs do, and it does a few things even better. There's feel and accuracy in the steering, plus balanced handling and a comfortable ride. Add to this the fierce acceleration from the big V8, which sees you hitting 60 mph in 8.7 seconds, and the ground clearance which makes it very practical off road, and the appeal of the Durango is obvious."

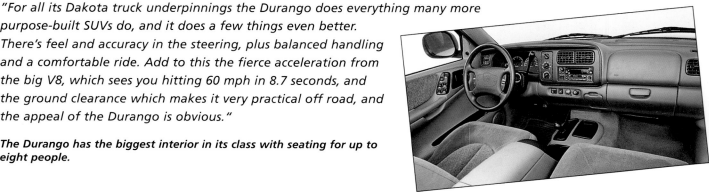

The Durango has the biggest interior in its class with seating for up to eight people.

Milestones

1986 Dodge
introduces the Dakota. Its first new mid-size truck, it fits in between the full-size D150 and the compact Ram. Two wheelbase lengths are available and engines start with the 2.2-liter four and include the 125-bhp 3.9-liter V6.

The Ramcharger was Dodge's only SUV for many years.

1996 A new Dakota
is launched. With an imposing style clearly inspired by the successful Ram, it is bigger and heavier than the 1980s version. Engines include a larger 2.5-liter four-cylinder, a 3.9-liter V6 and Magnum 5.2-liter V8.

The Durango gets its styling cues from the bigger Ram pickup.

1997 The Dakota
forms the basis of the new Durango. Engines start with the 3.9-liter V6, and the next step up is a 5.2-liter V8. The top of the range SLT Plus is powered by the 250-bhp, 5.9-liter V8.

UNDER THE SKIN

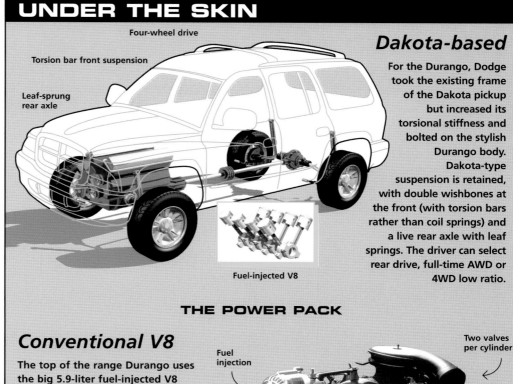

Four-wheel drive

Torsion bar front suspension

Leaf-sprung rear axle

Fuel-injected V8

Dakota-based

For the Durango, Dodge took the existing frame of the Dakota pickup but increased its torsional stiffness and bolted on the stylish Durango body. Dakota-type suspension is retained, with double wishbones at the front (with torsion bars rather than coil springs) and a live rear axle with leaf springs. The driver can select rear drive, full-time AWD or 4WD low ratio.

THE POWER PACK

Conventional V8

The top of the range Durango uses the big 5.9-liter fuel-injected V8 Magnum engine used by the Ramcharger. It has the traditional cast-iron block and heads, plus the usual two valves per cylinder operated by single V-mounted camshafts and hydraulic valve lifters. Over the years it has been given a little more power to bring it up to its current 250 bhp, but it is tuned for low rpm power (peaking at only 4,000 rpm) and torque, with all 335 lb-ft being on tap by 3,200 rpm.

Fuel injection

Two valves per cylinder

Cast-iron block and heads

Tuned for low-down power

Smaller V8

The Durango is good even without the mighty 5.9-liter V8 in the SLT Plus. The SLT, with a 5.2-liter version of the Magnum V8, has just 20 bhp and 35 lb-ft of torque less than the Plus model. It is a better bet than the 175-bhp, 3.9-liter V6 base model.

The Durango is one of the most striking SUVs in its class.

Dodge DURANGO 🇺🇸

Add a generous eight-seater body and a 250-bhp V8 engine to a truck chassis and you have the Durango SLT Plus—a carry-all SUV with the type of acceleration sports car owners used to brag about not all that long ago.

V8 engine

The fuel-injected 5.9-liter Magnum V8 is a short-stroke pushrod design with plenty of power and torque, but the all-iron construction helps to contribute to the Durango's front-heavy (56:44 front/rear) weight distribution.

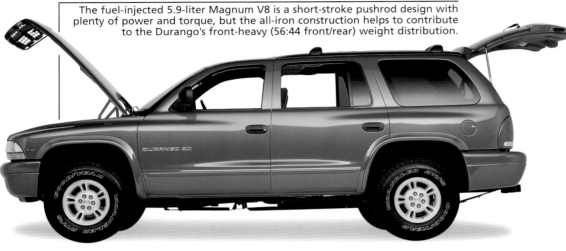

Four-speed automatic

There is no need to have a manual transmission with the 5.9-liter engine. The top of the range SLT Plus is fitted with a four-speed automatic with a high and relaxing overdrive.

Torsion bar front suspension

Dodge's long allegiance with torsion bar front suspension is continued in the Durango, in which the lower wishbones operate a torsion bar.

Separate chassis

Like all rugged trucks, the Durango is built on a separate chassis. The Durango's body is fixed to the frame with bolts and rubber bushings to help reduce noise and vibration.

High and low ratios

The driver only needs to select 'low' ratio in four-wheel drive in extreme circumstances. Creeping along at 3.4 mph per 1,000 revs, even a driver who is not skilled with the throttle is unlikely to spin the wheels on ice.

Specifications

1998 Dodge Durango SLT Plus

ENGINE

Type: V8

Construction: Cast-iron block and heads

Valve gear: Two valves per cylinder operated by a single V-mounted camshaft via pushrods, rockers and hydraulic tappets

Bore and stroke: 4.0 in.x 3.58 in.

Displacement: 5,898 cc

Compression ratio: 8.9:1

Induction system: Electronic port fuel injection

Maximum power: 250 bhp at 4,000 rpm

Maximum torque: 335 lb-ft at 3,200 rpm

Top speed: 115 mph

0–60 mph: 8.7 sec.

TRANSMISSION

Four-speed overdrive automatic transmission with selectable four-wheel drive in low and high ratio with lockable center differential

BODY/CHASSIS

Separate steel chassis frame with bolted-on steel four-door SUV body

SPECIAL FEATURES

The 5.9-liter V8 gives the Durango excellent performance.

The Durango is available in both two- and four-wheel drive versions.

RUNNING GEAR

Steering: Recirculating ball

Front suspension: Double wishbones with torsion bars, telescopic shock absorbers and anti-roll bar

Rear suspension: Live axle with leaf springs, telescopic shock absorbers and anti-roll bar

Brakes: Vented discs, 11.3-in. dia (front), drums, 11.0-in. dia (rear)

Wheels: Cast-aluminum alloy, 8 x 15 in.

Tires: 235/75 R15

DIMENSIONS

Length: 193.2 in.   **Width:** 71.5 in.

Height: 72.9 in.   **Wheelbase:** 115.9 in.

Track: 63.0 in. (front), 62.5 in. (rear)

Weight: 5,050 lbs.

Dodge LI'L RED EXPRESS TRUCK

Offered as a performance variant to Dodge's common full-size pickup truck, the Li'l Red Express with a 360 cubic-inch V8 as the standard engine was actually the fastest U.S. production vehicle in 1978. It is a true hot hauler in every sense of the term.

"...sense of authority."

"Sitting in the bucket seat behind the Tuff sport steering wheel and with a 225-bhp, 360-cubic inch V8 under foot, you have a commanding sense of authority on the road. The big, twin, chromed exhaust stacks behind the cab, the wide chrome wheels and the bold red and gold color represent a very 1970s image, but this truck's performance is definitely not 1970s. It rockets to 60 mph in just 6.6 seconds—faster than most contemporary cars."

For a pickup, the Li'l Red Express Truck is well equipped and quite civilized.

Milestones

1976 The Warlock is Chrysler's

first attempt at attracting young buyers of the fast growing light-duty truck market. This customized D-100 pickup is built from 1976 to 1979 in black, dark green or red with gold stripes.

The big Dodge Ram marched into the 1980s with few changes.

1978 The Li'l Red Express

attracts 2,188 buyers in its first year of production.

A new 'Big Rig'-styled Ram pickup arrived for 1994 and sales exploded.

1979 Production of the final Express

comes to an end after 5,118 have been built, bringing the total to 7,306. Quad rectangular headlights set it apart from the 1978 version. The basic Ram pickup on which it is based soldiers on until 1993.

UNDER THE SKIN

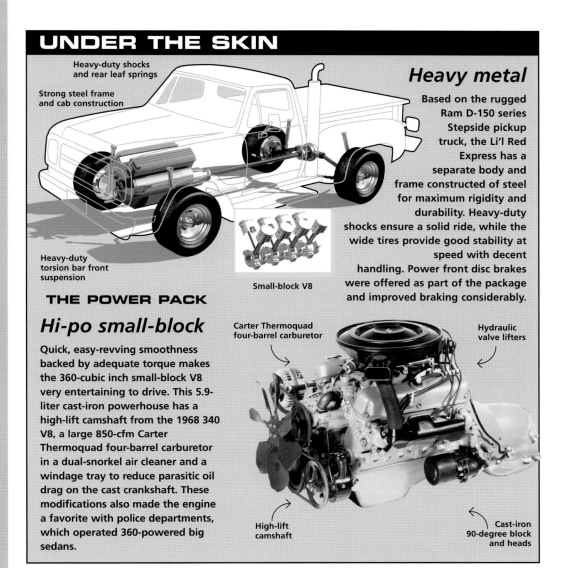

Heavy-duty shocks and rear leaf springs

Strong steel frame and cab construction

Heavy-duty torsion bar front suspension

Small-block V8

Heavy metal

Based on the rugged Ram D-150 series Stepside pickup truck, the Li'l Red Express has a separate body and frame constructed of steel for maximum rigidity and durability. Heavy-duty shocks ensure a solid ride, while the wide tires provide good stability at speed with decent handling. Power front disc brakes were offered as part of the package and improved braking considerably.

THE POWER PACK

Hi-po small-block

Quick, easy-revving smoothness backed by adequate torque makes the 360-cubic inch small-block V8 very entertaining to drive. This 5.9-liter cast-iron powerhouse has a high-lift camshaft from the 1968 340 V8, a large 850-cfm Carter Thermoquad four-barrel carburetor in a dual-snorkel air cleaner and a windage tray to reduce parasitic oil drag on the cast crankshaft. These modifications also made the engine a favorite with police departments, which operated 360-powered big sedans.

Carter Thermoquad four-barrel carburetor

Hydraulic valve lifters

High-lift camshaft

Cast-iron 90-degree block and heads

The heavy-duty bed is trimmed with wood.

Pre-emissions

The Li'l Red Express Truck was not the first Dodge 'factory custom' pickup, but it remains the best known. As far as collectability is concerned, the 1978 edition is slightly more desirable as fewer were built, plus 1978 was also the last year that light trucks were exempt from EPA emissions regulations and thus performance is marginally better than the 1979 version.

Dodge LI'L RED EXPRESS TRUCK

Ram pickups ordered with the Li'l Red Express Truck package are coded YH6. This includes the special engine, transmission and exhaust system, plus a wood-trimmed bed, chrome engine accessories and Canyon Red paint.

Smog equipment

This 1979 model is equipped with pollution control equipment, including a smog pump, EGR (Exhaust Gas Recirculating) system and catalytic converters. These power robbing devices aren't required on the 1978 models.

Heavy-duty suspension

In keeping with its performance image, heavy-duty shocks and rear leaf springs are fitted all around. Torsion bars control the front wheels.

Step side bed

Varnished solid oak side boards line the rugged step side steel bed and tailgate for added appeal.

Exhaust stacks

The eye-catching exhaust system is quite unique with its twin 2.5-inch chrome stacks exiting vertically behind the cab in a similar fashion to a giant 18-wheeler.

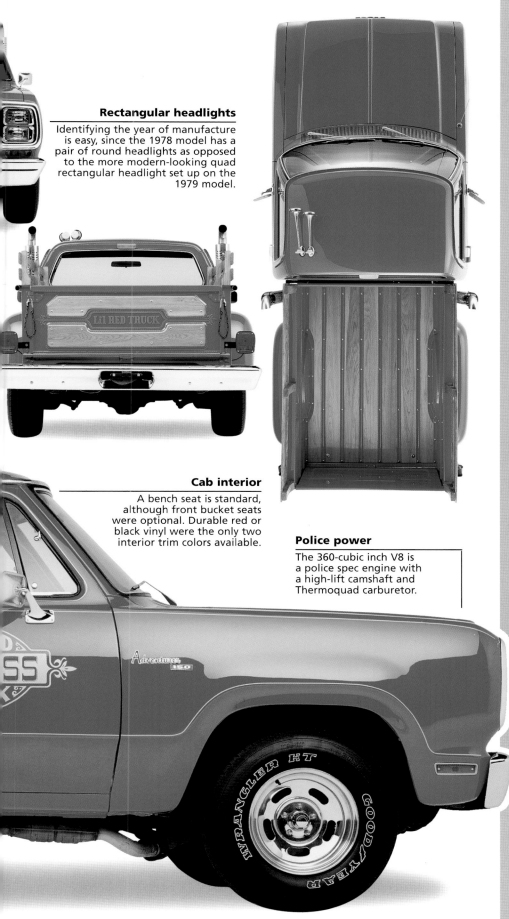

Rectangular headlights

Identifying the year of manufacture is easy, since the 1978 model has a pair of round headlights as opposed to the more modern-looking quad rectangular headlight set up on the 1979 model.

Cab interior

A bench seat is standard, although front bucket seats were optional. Durable red or black vinyl were the only two interior trim colors available.

Police power

The 360-cubic inch V8 is a police spec engine with a high-lift camshaft and Thermoquad carburetor.

Specifications

1979 Dodge Li'l Red Express Truck

ENGINE

Type: V8

Construction: Cast-iron block and heads

Valve gear: Two valves per cylinder operated by a single camshaft, pushrods, rockers and hydraulic lifters

Bore and stroke: 4.00 in. x 3.58 in.

Displacement: 360 c.i.

Compression ratio: 8.4:1

Induction system: Carter Thermoquad four-barrel carburetor

Maximum power: 225 bhp at 3,800 rpm

Maximum torque: 295 lb-ft at 3,200 rpm

Top speed: 118 mph

0–60 mph: 6.6 sec.

TRANSMISSION

Three-speed LoadFlite automatic

BODY/CHASSIS

Separate steel body and frame

SPECIAL FEATURES

The package even included an engine dress-up kit with a chrome air cleaner.

Li'l Red Express trucks were based on the Adventurer 150 series Ram.

RUNNING GEAR

Steering: Recirculating ball

Front suspension: Torsion bars with shock absorbers and anti-roll bar

Rear suspension: Live solid axle with leaf springs and shock absorbers

Brakes: Discs (front), drums (rear)

Wheels: 7 x 15 in.

Tires: GR60-15 (front), LR60-15 (rear)

DIMENSIONS

Length: 186.0 in.   **Width:** 76.0 in.

Height: 74.0 in.   **Wheelbase:** 115.0 in.

Track: 70.4 in. (front and rear)

Weight: 3,855 lbs.

Ford **MODEL 830 PICKUP**

Ford's passenger cars from the 1930s are probably the most famous hot rods, but the company's light trucks have just as much potential for modifications and, like this one, can be turned into equally head-turning mobile metal sculptures.

"...a run for the money."

"In stock form, the Model 830 Pickup is a charming but very basic machine. This one, with luxurious front bucket seats, a soft ride and air conditioning, is anything but. A 350 Chevy crate motor coupled to a TH350 automatic transmission means it can give many late-model sports cars a run for their money in straight-line acceleration contests. But, this custom-hauler is best used for engaging in the time-honored tradition of cruising along the boulevard, showing off its sleek lines."

Ford Motorsport SVO gauges, a billet steering wheel and color-coded upholstery piping add a touch of class.

Milestones

1932 Like regular Ford passenger cars,
the light truck line receives a smoother front grill and smaller wheels. New are the Model BB 1- and 1½-ton truck chassis and the 221-cubic inch Flathead V8. This engine is not available in commercial vehicles until late in the year, so most pickups have four-cylinder engines.

Many earlier pickups, like this Model A, have convertible tops.

1933 Styling is altered
only in detail on Ford light trucks. The ½-ton pickup is offered with either closed or open cabs.

The 1935 pickup closely mirrors the 1933/34-model 40/40A passenger cars in its styling.

1934 The open-cab
option is discontinued.

1935 Major changes
include a more streamlined body and the engine is positioned 8 inches farther forward.

UNDER THE SKIN

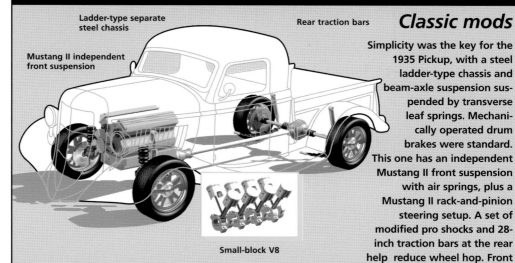

Ladder-type separate steel chassis

Mustang II independent front suspension

Rear traction bars

Small-block V8

Classic mods

Simplicity was the key for the 1935 Pickup, with a steel ladder-type chassis and beam-axle suspension suspended by transverse leaf springs. Mechanically operated drum brakes were standard. This one has an independent Mustang II front suspension with air springs, plus a Mustang II rack-and-pinion steering setup. A set of modified pro shocks and 28-inch traction bars at the rear help reduce wheel hop. Front disc brakes aid in stopping.

THE POWER PACK

Crate eight

A single engine powered light-duty Ford trucks in 1935: the 221-cubic inch flathead V8. With a 6.3:1 compression ratio and a single two-barrel carburetor, it produced 85 bhp and made these rigs quite quick for the day. Although the Flathead became the engine of choice, it was later supplanted by the small-block Chevy V8, a version of which is found in this particular truck. The 1997 350-cubic inch GM Performance Parts Crate motor features a cast-iron block, aluminum heads and intake manifold, plus a Holley 650-cfm four-barrel carburetor. The power output of 320 bhp at 5,400 rpm reduces its speed to 60 mph in 6.4 seconds.

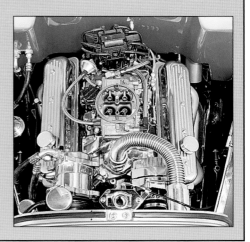

Interchange

With 42,763 examples built in 1935, the Model 830 Pickup was quite popular in its day. Simple engineering and shared parts with the Model 48 passenger car mean that it is also the ideal basis for a truly unique and stylish street rod.

Quick, stylish and practical, this Model 830 Pickup has it all.

Ford **MODEL 830 PICKUP**

It may not look ultra-radical, but this 1935 Ford Model 830 Pickup street rod has many subtle touches. And with its small-block V8 and modern rubber, it is also one killer cruising machine.

Smoother box
An extra panel was fitted between the running boards and pickup box for 1935. This resulted in a smoother, more integrated look.

Traction ba...
A live ax...
suspended ...
leaf springs ...
found at the rea...
but wi...
360 lb-ft ...
torque bei...
transmitted ...
the rear whee...
good bite off th...
line is essentia...
This is improve...
by 28-in...
traction bar...

Mustang II front suspension
A favorite with rodders, the Mustang II front clip is easy to weld onto just about any street rod. Gas-filled shocks and air springs give this 830 Pickup improved handling and a better ride compared to that of many other street rods.

Deluxe interior
In 1935, a front bench seat was the only concession to luxury in the Model 830 Pickup. The interior of this one, with its leather-upholstered front bucket seats, Motorsport SVO gauges, air conditioning and Sony stereo system, is nothing like the way the interior came from the factory in 1935.

Beefy wheels and tires

One of the biggest handling improvements that can be made to a car are upgraded wheels and tires. A set of Budnik billet-aluminum rims really looks the part on this pickup and, shod with low-profile Dunlop Sport 8000 tires, ensures that this truck is able to hold its own on the road.

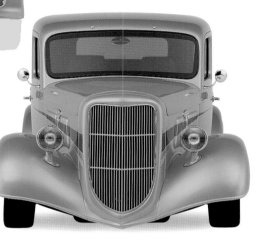

Candy color

In the 1960s, candy and metal-flake paint schemes were very stylish. This 1990s rod has a custom-mixed Candy Pearl Orange hue.

1935 Ford Model 830 Pickup

ENGINE

Type: V8

Construction: Cast-iron block and heads

Valve gear: Two valves per cylinder operated by a single V-mounted camshaft with pushrods and rockers

Bore and stroke: 4.00 in. x 3.48 in.

Displacement: 350 c.i.

Compression ratio: 9.5:1

Induction system: Holley 650-cfm four-barrel downdraft carburetor

Maximum power: 320 bhp at 5,400 rpm

Maximum torque: 360 lb-ft at 3,800 rpm

Top speed: 110 mph

0–60 mph: 6.4 sec.

TRANSMISSION

TH350 three-speed automatic

BODY/CHASSIS

Separate steel chassis with steel and fiberglass pickup body

SPECIAL FEATURES

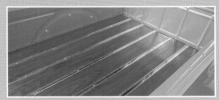

A wooden floor with chrome accents is popular with the custom truck crowd.

Separate rear fenders were standard on most light trucks of the 1930s.

RUNNING GEAR

Steering: Rack-and-pinion

Front suspension: Unequal-length A-arms with air springs, telescopic shock absorbers and anti-roll bar

Rear suspension: Live axle with semi-elliptic leaf springs and telescopic shock absorbers

Brakes: Discs (front), drums (rear)

Wheels: Budnik Billet, 8 x 17 in. (front), 9.5 x 18 in. (rear)

Tires: Dunlop SP Sport 8000

DIMENSIONS

Length: 157.5 in. **Width:** 70.6 in.

Height: 63.5 in.   **Wheelbase:** 112.0 in

Track: 50.7 in. (front), 56.8 in. (rear)

Weight: 3,280 lbs.

Ford FALCON RANCHERO

Adopting the compact Falcon platform in 1960, the Ranchero continued to tempt those who were looking for a recreational pickup truck. The V8 powerplant, light weight and unitary chassis all helped to make these vehicles excellent alternatives for those into modified cars.

"...no ordinary Ranchero."

"Rancheros were always among the most spartan Falcon derivatives, and this one maintains that theme. It has a front bench seat and a horizontal sweep speedometer, but the Grant steering wheel and aftermarket tach indicate that this is no ordinary Ranchero. Modern small-block power means this truck is a great daily driver, with ample power to spare. It will sprint to 60 mph in less than eight seconds, but the fun does not stop there —it can stop and take corners, too."

Grant GT steering wheel and tach give an almost competition feel to the cabin.

Milestones

1960 Ranchero transfers
to the new compact Falcon chassis and is advertised as 'America's lowest price pickup' retailing for just $1,882. Powered by a 144-cubic inch, 90-bhp six, 21,027 are built.

Falcon got its first major restyling and V8 power for the 1964 model year.

1964 The Falcon gets a
facelift, as does the Ranchero. A 200-cubic inch six and a 260-cubic inch V8 are options.

1965 would mark the last year for the Falcon Ranchero.

1965 A new grill with a
center divider and revised trim marks this year's Ranchero. Performance gets a boost in the shape of two 289-cubic inch V8s, the latter boasting an Autolite four-barrel carb and 225 bhp. Production of Falcon-based Rancheros reaches 10,539 this year.

1966 Ranchero adopts
the mid-size chassis.

UNDER THE SKIN

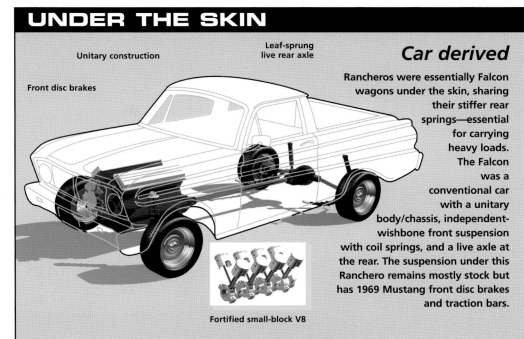

Unitary construction

Leaf-sprung live rear axle

Front disc brakes

Fortified small-block V8

Car derived

Rancheros were essentially Falcon wagons under the skin, sharing their stiffer rear springs—essential for carrying heavy loads. The Falcon was a conventional car with a unitary body/chassis, independent-wishbone front suspension with coil springs, and a live axle at the rear. The suspension under this Ranchero remains mostly stock but has 1969 Mustang front disc brakes and traction bars.

THE POWER PACK

Modern update

Early Falcons were powered exclusively by six-cylinder engines, though beginning in 1964, V8s began finding their way under the hood. This particular car originally came with a 200-bhp, 289, two-barrel V8, but this is long gone. A 1980 302-cubic inch small block has taken the original power plant's place. This engine, an outgrowth of the 289, originally produced just 130 bhp and 222 lb-ft of torque, but thanks to an Edelbrock Performer camshaft, intake manifold and carburetor, a recurved distributor, Heddman free-flow exhaust headers and Flowmaster mufflers, it puts out considerably more power—200 bhp and 285 lb-ft of torque.

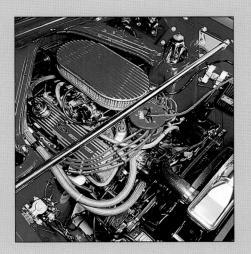

Most athletic

Trimmest, and offering perhaps the greatest performance potential of all Rancheros, the Falcon-based pickup can be had for a very reasonable price today, and with the right modifications it can make for an excellent yet distinctive daily driver.

Based on its styling, the 1965 model is perhaps the nicest Ranchero of all.

Ford FALCON RANCHERO

The original car-based pickup, the Ranchero uncovered a new market during the late 1950s and early 1960s. Although it has been long out of production, it is still a well-respected cruising vehicle.

Later engine
Replacing the original 289 is a version of its successor, the 302. This one has been fitted with a classic 1960s-style chrome dress-up kit, but modern enhancements such as an Edelbrock intake and carburetor ensure that it is less temperamental and produces more power than a comparable 1960s engine.

Free-flowing exhaust
This Ranchero has been fitted with tubular Heddman headers and full-length dual Flowmaster pipes, resulting in a wonderful sound and quick 0-60 mph acceleration.

Stiffer suspension
Compared to standard Falcon sedans, Rancheros have stiffer rear springs in order to cope with the heavier loads. This means that hot-rodded versions suffer from poor weight transfer and traction with the bed unloaded. This problem has been cured somewhat on this car by using traction bars on the rear leaf springs.

Stock body
Virtually stock, the only modifications made to the body have been a respray in PPG Burgundy Pearl paint and the addition of a pair of 1969 Fairlane exterior door mirrors.

In view of performance

To improve torsional stiffness, this Ranchero has a shock-tower brace and stiffener between the fenders. This helps it handle much better than a similar stock example.

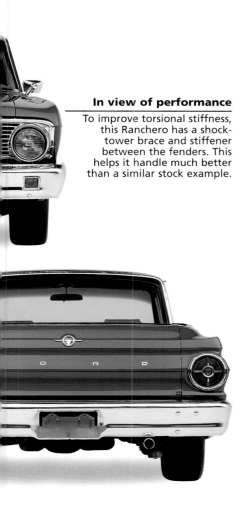

Late-model rubber

Tire technology has improved handling and grip beyond all other modifications since the 1960s. BF Goodrich radials feature a meaty 8 x 15 inches at the front and 10 x 15 inches at the back.

Specifications

1965 Ford Falcon Ranchero

ENGINE
Type: V8

Construction: Cast-iron block and heads

Valve gear: Two valves per cylinder operated by pushrods and rockers

Bore and stroke: 4.00 in. x 3.00 in.

Displacement: 302 c.i.

Compression ratio: 9.5:1

Induction system: Edelbrock Performer four-barrel carburetor

Maximum power: 200 bhp at 4,400 rpm

Maximum torque: 285 lb-ft at 3,200 rpm

Top speed: 120 mph

0–60 mph: 7.4 sec.

TRANSMISSION
Borg Warner T-10 four-speed manual

BODY/CHASSIS
Steel unitary chassis with two-door pickup body

SPECIAL FEATURES

Fender badges signify this Ranchero originally came with a 289-c.i. V8.

Centerline billet wheels add a 1990s theme to this custom pickup.

RUNNING GEAR
Steering: Recirculating ball

Front suspension: Unequal-length A-arms with coil springs, telescopic shock absorbers and stabilizer bar

Rear suspension: Live axle with semi-elliptic leaf springs, traction bars and telescopic shock absorbers

Brakes: 9.5-in. discs (front), 9.0-in. drums (rear)

Wheels: Centerline billet, 8 x 15 in. (front), 10 x 15 in. (rear)

Tires: BF Goodrich, 15-in. dia.

DIMENSIONS
Length: 190.0 in.   **Width:** 71.6 in.

Height: 54.2 in.   **Wheelbase:** 109.5 in.

Track: 55.9 in. (front), 53.3 in. (rear)

Weight: 2,820 lbs.

Ford F1

One of the most significant trucks of the early postwar period, the Ford F-1 offered a spacious interior, V8 power and rugged simplicity. More than 50 years later, it remains an important piece of U.S. motoring history.

"...puts others to shame."

"Pull open the door and slide on in. In place of the original seat is a modern Ford Ranger split bench, giving you far greater comfort than anyone imagined back in 1948. With a 351 Windsor under the bulbous hood, this well-built Ford pulls extremely well off the line and the tires really dig in. When turning corners, this rig will put many new trucks to shame, despite its primitive underpinnings. Overall, it is a very attractive and eye-catching vehicle."

Full gauges and an adjustable split bench—this F-1 never had it so good.

Milestones

1948 The first postwar
Ford vehicle, the F-1, goes on sale. It has new styling as well as a taller and wider cab and greater refinement. The standard engine is a 226 L-head six, but the 239.4-cubic inch flathead V8 is a popular option.

The F-1 was replaced by the F-100 in 1953.

1949 Running boards bolted
to the frame rails and slight trim changes distinguish this year's F-1. The light truck range proves popular this year and 138,000 are built.

Today, the Ford F-series pickup is the world's best-selling vehicle.

1951 After a carryover
of the 1950 model, this year the F-1 has a new grill and pickup box. The engines get sturdy bottom ends, waterproof ignition and a stronger transmission arrives.

UNDER THE SKIN

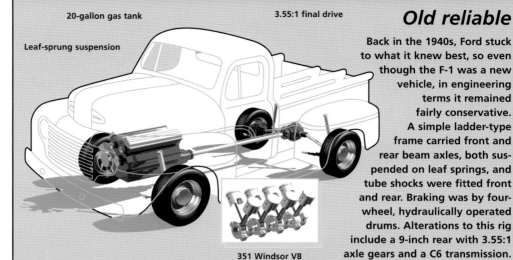

20-gallon gas tank

3.55:1 final drive

Leaf-sprung suspension

351 Windsor V8

Old reliable

Back in the 1940s, Ford stuck to what it knew best, so even though the F-1 was a new vehicle, in engineering terms it remained fairly conservative. A simple ladder-type frame carried front and rear beam axles, both suspended on leaf springs, and tube shocks were fitted front and rear. Braking was by four-wheel, hydraulically operated drums. Alterations to this rig include a 9-inch rear with 3.55:1 axle gears and a C6 transmission.

THE POWER PACK

Windsor power

When introduced as a 1948 model, the F-1 stuck with the proven Ford L-head six as the standard engine, and the flathead V8 was optional. With a 6.2:1 compression ratio and 100 bhp on tap, the old V8 was not exactly a high-performance engine but did make the F-1 faster than many rivals of the day. For a little more kick, the owner of this rig decided to replace the flathead with a 1969 vintage 351-cubic inch Windsor. Sporting a four-barrel Holley 600-cfm carburetor and a fully balanced rotating assembly, the V8 produces in the region of 275 bhp, putting the truck truly in the performance league.

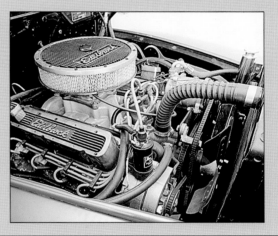

Custom cool

In the 1970s, few people were interested in old trucks, but as the price of collectible cars began to rise in the 1980s, classic rigs, like the F-1, began to gain collector interest. These old trucks are popular with the street custom crowd, too.

Ford F-1s are among the most popular postwar trucks today.

Ford F-1

Solid, dependable, but hardly sporty, the stock F-1 has timeless appeal and considerable scope for hot-rodding. This one combines nostalgic appeal with modern comfort and performance.

351 Windsor V8
In place of the old flathead is what became its spiritual successor and the powerplant for millions of Ford trucks. The 351-cubic inch Windsor has been fully balanced, blueprinted and can push this F-1 to 60 mph in 8.7 seconds.

Floored fen
In the late 1940s, Ford st
was one of gradual evolu
Stylist E.T. 'Bob' Gre
concentrated on sm
curves, giving the F-1 a
integrated look, not u
its predecessor, the Mode

Dropped front suspension
Lowering blocks on the front springs give this truck an aggressive stance, which is routine for modified street pickups.

Pearl and teal

'Cool' paint colors have gained popularity in recent years as an alternative to the high-impact hues that adorn so many custom vehicles. This F-1 has a teal metallic lower body paint, with upper surfaces finished in contrasting pearl metallic. A clever touch is the flames and ghost scallops.

Stainless-steel bed

One of the neatest tricks on the F-1 is the bed. It has a stainless-steel floor with custom-built side boards mounted above the bed. These are made from an aluminum base with oak inserts for a classic touch.

Specifications
1948 Ford F-1

ENGINE
Type: V8

Construction: Cast-iron block and heads

Valve gear: Two valves per cylinder operated by a single V-mounted camshaft with pushrods and rockers

Bore and stroke: 4.00 in. x 3.50 in.

Displacement: 351 c.i.

Compression ratio: 9.5:1

Induction system: Holley four-barrel carburetor

Maximum power: 275 bhp at 4,800 rpm

Maximum torque: 380 lb-ft at 3,400 rpm

Top speed: 105 mph

0–60 mph: 8.7 sec.

TRANSMISSION
C6 three-speed automatic

BODY/CHASSIS
Separate steel chassis with steel cab and bed

SPECIAL FEATURES

Attention to detail is apparent in the stainless-steel custom painted bed.

A small fire extinguisher is mounted on the left side of cab in case of emergency.

RUNNING GEAR
Steering: Recirculating-ball

Front suspension: Beam axle with semi-elliptic leaf springs and telescopic shock absorbers

Rear suspension: Live axle with semi-elliptic leaf springs and telescopic shock absorbers

Brakes: Drums (front and rear)

Wheels: Steel, 15-in. dia.

Tires: Goodyear Aquatread

DIMENSIONS
Length: 177.8 in.   **Width:** 77.7 in.

Height: 70.6 in.   **Wheelbase:** 114.0 in.

Track: 65.5 in. (front and rear)

Weight: 3,120 lbs.

Ford **F-100**

When it comes to classic trucks, the 1956 Ford F-100 stands out. It was one of the most powerful and fastest trucks in its day and was also one of the first to achieve cult status.

"...straight back to the 1950s."

"Driving this truck is an experience in itself. The interior takes you straight back to the 1950s, as does the rumpity sound of the vintage Y-block that is nourished by three Stromberg two-barrel carburetors. The ride may still be a bit bumpy with the bed unloaded, but the F-100 is quick off the line and feels faster still, thanks to the manual transmission. The original suspension has been retained, but a custom lowering kit brings its belly closer to the ground."

Sliding behind the wheel is like stepping through a time warp.

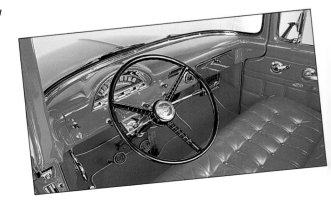

Milestones

1953 Introduced
in March, the new F-100 replaces the 1948-vintage F-1. It has all-new styling and a set-back front axle. A larger cab and improved suspension set new standards in pickup comfort and refinement. Powered by inline six or flathead V8 engines, a total of 116,437 are built.

The 1948-vintage F-1 got a new grill for the 1951 model year.

1954 A new Y-block overhead-valve V8
replaces the flathead. Known as the Power King, it is rated at 130 bhp and 214 lb-ft of torque.

Today, the F-series truck is the world's best-selling vehicle.

1956 The cab is restyled
with a wraparound windshield, which alters its appearance. A 12-volt electrical system and a 273-cubic inch 'Power King' V8 debut. A 10.5-inch clutch is standard on all V8 F-100s. A new F-series truck arrives for the 1957 model year.

UNDER THE SKIN

Separate ladder-type chassis

Ford 9-inch differential

Lowered front suspension

Y-block V8

Show and go
Ford trucks of this era are simple, rugged machines, with a ladder-type chassis frame and leaf-sprung suspension. Modifications on this F-100 include a lowered front end, a 1968 Ford rear axle with a nine-inch differential and 2.75:1 gearing. Also added are power front disc brakes, stainless-steel nuts and fuel lines, and a custom chromed exhaust system.

THE POWER PACK

True Power King

In 1952, Ford introduced an overhead-valve V8. This engine was available in Ford trucks from 1954, and by 1956 it was up to 272-cubic inches. This Ford has been fitted with a fully balanced and blueprinted Mercury engine that now has a displacement of 296 cubic inches. Big 312 headers help the V8 exhale, plus a custom ground crank and Magnafluxed rods help improve upper rpm power. An Edelbrock intake topped with three Stromberg carburetors helps breathing.

Three Stromberg carburetors

Edelbrock intake manifold

.030-inch overbore

9.2:1 compression ratio

Red hot roller

Collector interest in the 1956 F-100 has been very strong for a long time, and a ready supply of parts are available for these trucks. The classic styling and V8 power both respond well to custom modifications, and prices are reasonable compared to cars.

Although made in substantial numbers, the 1956 F-100 is coveted today.

Ford **F-100**

Packing considerable power even in stock trim, and with timeless looks and simple yet sturdy mechanics, the 1956 F-100 truly deserves the title of all-time classic pickup truck.

Worked Y-block

A larger Mercury unit replaces the stock 272-cubic inch V8. It has been overbored by .030-inch and has an Iskendarian high-lift camshaft, Magnafluxed connecting rods, Edelbrock intake and triple Stromberg carburetors. It puts out an impressive 300 bhp at only 4,500 rpm.

Classic-style exhaust

Spent gases from the engine are exhaled through a custom exhaust system. The system gives an unmistakable, throaty, nostalgic sound.

Lowered nose

A set-back front axle gives these trucks a nose-in-the-weeds stance. Customizers often accentuate this look even further. This F-100 has been lowered by two inches, which improves handling, too.

Attention to detail

It may not appear radical on the outside, but this F-100 has many clever touches. The brake and fuel lines are steel braided, and every nut and bolt on the entire vehicle has been replaced with stainless steel hardware. The taillight wires are covered in chromed flexible tubing.

Wraparound rear window

A flat back window was standard on F-100s in 1956, but a wraparound piece was available as an option. If ordered, the buyer also got chrome windshield moldings. Few were fitted, making F-100s with this item very rare today.

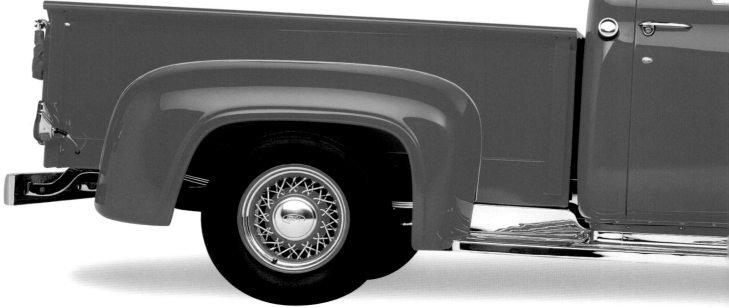

Stepside bed

One of the reasons these trucks are so popular today is the Stepside bed and full running boards. (1957 saw the introduction of the full bed—sheet metal flush with the cab.) Stepside trucks are not as practical, but in modified form they look much better than the full-bed versions.

Quality interior

The leather used on the bench seat was sent to England to be dye-matched to the interior colors of red and orange on the door panels. Real wool was used for the interior carpet.

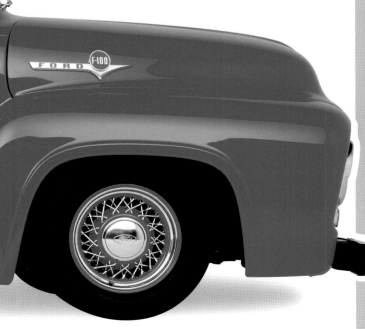

Specifications
1956 Ford F-100

ENGINE

Type: V8

Construction: Cast-iron block and heads

Valve gear: Two valves per cylinder operated by a single camshaft via pushrods and rockers

Bore and stroke: 3.78 in. x 3.30 in.

Displacement: 296 c.i.

Compression ratio: 9.2:1

Induction system: Three Stromberg two-barrel carburetors

Maximum power: 300 bhp at 4,500 rpm

Maximum torque: 270 lb-ft at 2,300 rpm

Top speed: 110 mph

0–60 mph: 8.1 sec.

TRANSMISSION

Three-speed manual

BODY/CHASSIS

Separate ladder-type steel chassis with steel cab and bed

SPECIAL FEATURES

V8-powered F-100s are identified by big grill badges. Sixes did without.

Chrome is used extensively underneath, including the shocks and differential.

RUNNING GEAR

Steering: Recirculating ball

Front suspension: Beam axle with semi-elliptic leaf springs and telescopic shock absorbers

Rear suspension: Live axle with semi-elliptic leaf springs and telescopic shock absorbers

Brakes: Discs (front), drums (rear)

Wheels: Sharp Spoke wire, 15-in. dia.

Tires: BF Goodrich, 15-in. dia.

DIMENSIONS

Length: 212.0 in. **Width:** 59.3 in.

Height: 80.9 in. **Wheelbase:** 114.0 in.

Track: 49.0 in. (front), 48.2 in. (rear)

Weight: 3,175 lbs.

Ford **F-150 LIGHTNING**

Muscle trucks were big in the early 1990s. To counter the opposition, Ford's Special Vehicle Team (SVT) took the standard short-bed F-150 and transformed it into the potent Lightning—a true performance machine that is also completely practical.

"...lusty acceleration."

"Governed by a limiter that restricts top speed to 120 mph, the Lightning is nevertheless a blast. Its has lusty acceleration: stab the throttle to the floor and this heavyweight monster reaches 60 mph in just 7.5 seconds. Shifts in the four-speed automatic are super smooth, and thanks to a specially-developed suspension and fat rubber, it handles much better than you'd think. However, with its live axle, the tail needs watching in the wet."

Fairly sober, the Lightning boasts power windows and door locks, plus cruise control.

Milestones

1975 The F-150 is introduced. It is a heavy-duty variant of the standard F-100 pickup and has a greater payload and towing capacity. 300-, 390- and 460-cubic inch V8s are offered.

Ford SVT's first performance car was the 1993 Mustang Cobra.

1981 All-new, smaller and lighter
F-series models, with slightly more modern styling, are launched. Although fitted with smaller V8s, an even larger range of equipment is available.

1992 The F series receives a moderate facelift and a revised interior. It is becomes a best seller for Ford.

Standard F-150s are offered in numerous configurations.

1993 A hot-rodded Lightning version appears.

1994 White joins black and red as exterior color options for the Lightning.

UNDER THE SKIN

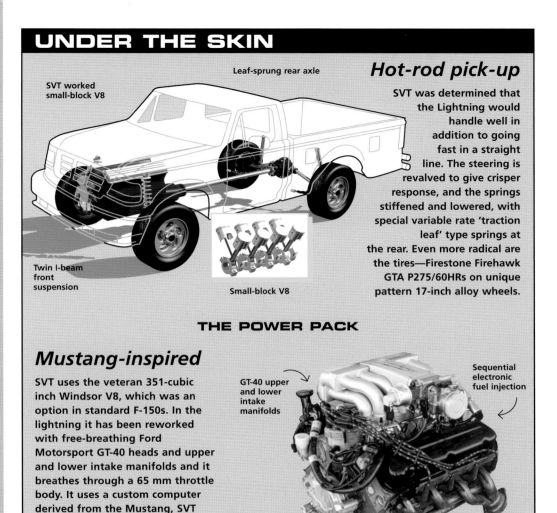

Leaf-sprung rear axle

SVT worked small-block V8

Twin I-beam front suspension

Small-block V8

Hot-rod pick-up

SVT was determined that the Lightning would handle well in addition to going fast in a straight line. The steering is revalved to give crisper response, and the springs stiffened and lowered, with special variable rate 'traction leaf' type springs at the rear. Even more radical are the tires—Firestone Firehawk GTA P275/60HRs on unique pattern 17-inch alloy wheels.

THE POWER PACK

Mustang-inspired

SVT uses the veteran 351-cubic inch Windsor V8, which was an option in standard F-150s. In the lightning it has been reworked with free-breathing Ford Motorsport GT-40 heads and upper and lower intake manifolds and it breathes through a 65 mm throttle body. It uses a custom computer derived from the Mustang, SVT lightning-specific camshaft and tubular stainless-steel exhaust manifolds. These modifications help make the engine's 240 bhp.

GT-40 upper and lower intake manifolds

Sequential electronic fuel injection

Cast-iron block and cylinder heads

Aluminum pistons

Sure bet

During the four-year period in which Lightnings were built, the only change was the addition of a driver's airbag in 1994. Many Lightnings have been cherished by their owners and are a great buy— a full-size pickup that drives like a performance car.

The Lightning offers both practicality and performance.

Ford **F-150 LIGHTNING**

Incorporating the same ingredients used in the 5.0-liter Mustang, Ford's Special Vehicle Team worked its magic on the stock Ford F-150 and turned it into a real fire-breathing performance truck.

Old-fashioned V8

Introduced in 1968, the 351-cubic inch Windsor V8 was old-tech to say the least. Thanks to new cylinder heads and intake and larger exhaust ports and manifolds, it puts out a healthy 240 bhp.

Lowered to improve handling

Dropping the vehicle and adding fat Firestone tires gives the Lightning a much more aggressive stance than a regular F-150.

Beefed-up drivetrain

To cope with the increased torque of the V8, the Lightning has a massaged E4OD automatic transmission with its own oil cooler. The driveshaft is made from lightweight aluminum.

Rear-wheel drive

The Lightning's 8.8 inch rear is equipped with 4.10:1 gears to exploit its sweltering acceleration capabilities.

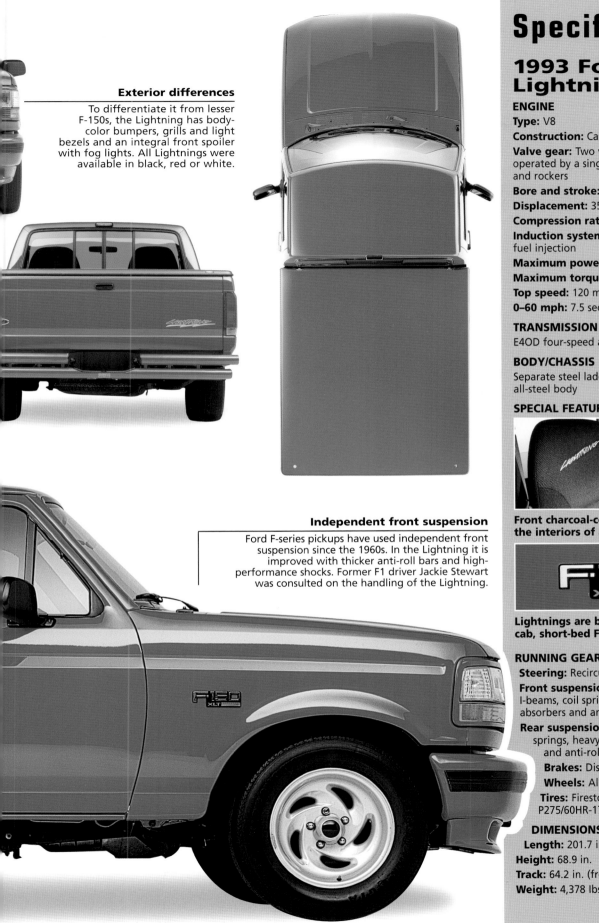

Exterior differences

To differentiate it from lesser F-150s, the Lightning has body-color bumpers, grills and light bezels and an integral front spoiler with fog lights. All Lightnings were available in black, red or white.

Independent front suspension

Ford F-series pickups have used independent front suspension since the 1960s. In the Lightning it is improved with thicker anti-roll bars and high-performance shocks. Former F1 driver Jackie Stewart was consulted on the handling of the Lightning.

Specifications

1993 Ford F-150 Lightning

ENGINE

Type: V8

Construction: Cast-iron block and heads

Valve gear: Two valves per cylinder operated by a single camshaft via pushrods and rockers

Bore and stroke: 4.00 in. x 3.50 in.

Displacement: 351 c.i.

Compression ratio: 8.8:1

Induction system: Sequential electronic fuel injection

Maximum power: 240 bhp at 4,200 rpm

Maximum torque: 340 lb-ft at 3,200 rpm

Top speed: 120 mph

0–60 mph: 7.5 sec.

TRANSMISSION

E4OD four-speed automatic with overdrive

BODY/CHASSIS

Separate steel ladder-type chassis with all-steel body

SPECIAL FEATURES

Front charcoal-colored buckets garnish the interiors of all Lightnings.

Lightnings are based on the regular cab, short-bed F-150 XLT.

RUNNING GEAR

Steering: Recirculating ball

Front suspension: Independent twin I-beams, coil springs, heavy-duty shock absorbers and anti-roll bar.

Rear suspension: Live axle with leaf springs, heavy-duty shock absorbers and anti-roll bar.

Brakes: Discs (front), drums (rear)

Wheels: Alloy, 17-in. dia.

Tires: Firestone Firehawk GTA, P275/60HR-17

DIMENSIONS

Length: 201.7 in.   **Width:** 79 in.

Height: 68.9 in.   **Wheelbase:** 116.8 in.

Track: 64.2 in. (front), 63.5 in. (rear)

Weight: 4,378 lbs.

Ford **F-150**

Ford's F-150 pickup is currently America's best-selling vehicle. It offers the brute strength and power of a traditional pickup, yet can be specified with comfort and convenience options most often found in luxury cars.

"...outstanding refinement."

"With each passing redesign, the F-150 becomes more car-like. The current truck offers a comfortable front bench seat with a well-designed dashboard and easy-to-use controls. The 5.4-liter Triton V8 is quiet and refined but offers spades of low-down torque, making light work of passing giant 18-wheelers. Best of all though, the level of refinement is outstanding for a full-size pickup; there's a smooth ride with minimal vibration and wind noise."

The smart, car-like cabin is comfortable and offers plenty of storage.

Milestones

1995 With the F-150 established as the best selling vehicle in the U.S., Ford begins production of a brand new model. It has smooth car-like styling and an improved interior. It proves to be very popular, although the old F-150 remains in production alongside the new truck for a few months.

By the 1970s, F-150s were becoming more civilized.

1998 The new F-250 and F-350 Super Duty trucks have distinctly different styling than the F-150. Two new engines arrive in the shape of a 5.4-liter Triton V8 and a 6.8-liter V10.

Larger Super Duty F-series trucks are more powerful and rugged than the current F-150.

1999 Still top of the sales charts, the F-150 receives a fourth door option on the Supercab and an increase in power from 210 to 260 bhp for the 5.4-liter V8.

UNDER THE SKIN

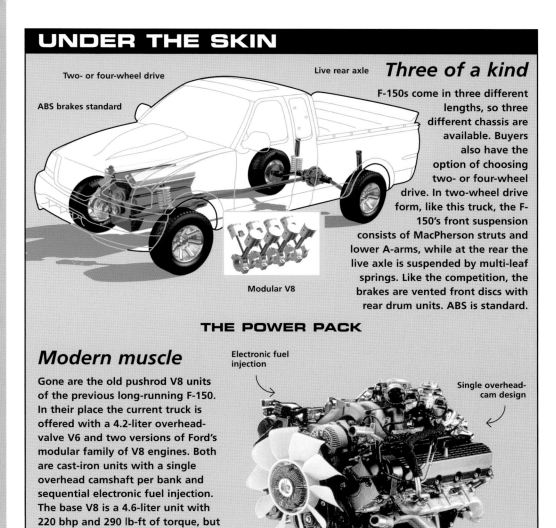

Two- or four-wheel drive

ABS brakes standard

Live rear axle

Modular V8

Three of a kind

F-150s come in three different lengths, so three different chassis are available. Buyers also have the option of choosing two- or four-wheel drive. In two-wheel drive form, like this truck, the F-150's front suspension consists of MacPherson struts and lower A-arms, while at the rear the live axle is suspended by multi-leaf springs. Like the competition, the brakes are vented front discs with rear drum units. ABS is standard.

THE POWER PACK

Modern muscle

Gone are the old pushrod V8 units of the previous long-running F-150. In their place the current truck is offered with a 4.2-liter overhead-valve V6 and two versions of Ford's modular family of V8 engines. Both are cast-iron units with a single overhead camshaft per bank and sequential electronic fuel injection. The base V8 is a 4.6-liter unit with 220 bhp and 290 lb-ft of torque, but the larger 5.4-liter Triton unit is proving to be a popular upgrade. It turns the light-duty truck into a strong all-around performer.

Electronic fuel injection

Single overhead-cam design

Cast-iron block

5.4 liters

V8 value

As an everyday, on-road vehicle, the Supercab, short-bed, two-wheel drive version is probably the most practical. The optional 5.4-liter V8 is also worth considering, with its extra power and torque. This is this the best value for the money.

A special Dale Jarret Limited Edition package became available in late 1998.

Ford **F-150**

With its smooth, contemporary exterior, combined with refined, torquey engines and a spacious, comfortable cab, it is easy to see why the F-150 remains one of the most rugged full-size pickups.

High-tech engines

Although an overhead-valve 4.2-liter V6 is the standard engine, the vast majority of F-150s are powered by overhead-cam V8s. Initially, the 4.6-liter unit was the only option, but a larger 5.4-liter engine arrived for 1997 and has proved tremendously popular thanks to its additional power and torque.

Borla dual exhaust

Dual exhaust offers significant performance gains. This truck is fitted with a Borla system. It's regarded as one of the best in the aftermarket.

Locking rear tailgate

A first for a full-size truck, the F-150 offers a locking rear tailgate. This prevents the door swinging open without warning and deters thieves from stealing the bed's contents.

Two-wheel drive suspension

In two-wheel drive form, this F-150 has independent front suspension with coil springs. At the rear is a live axle with 3.55:1 gears, suspended by multi-leaf springs. Front vented disc brakes and ABS are fitted to this particular truck.

Heavy-duty chassis

Despite being classified as a light truck, the F-150 still has plenty of hard-wearing items such as a rigid ladder-frame chassis. Extra rubber bushings result in a ride and stiffness which is on par with many unibody vehicles.

Dale Jarret Limited Edition package

This package, named after one of Ford's most successful NASCAR racers, includes special graphics by Down Force, a unique steel cowl-induction hood, a rear roll pan and cowl cover, special power moonroof, tonneau cover, ULTRA aluminum wheels and a Borla exhaust system.

Extra doors

A few years ago, big, extended-cab pickups were difficult to get into at the rear. All this has changed with the addition of rearward-hinging doors. A third door was offered on the F-150 beginning in 1996, but dual rear doors are now available, giving unparalleled access to the rear seats.

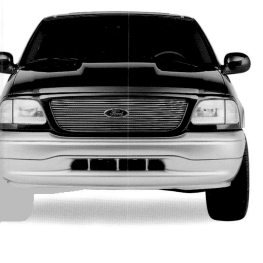

Specifications

1999 Ford F-150 XLT

ENGINE
Type: V8
Construction: Cast-iron block and heads
Valve gear: Two valves per cylinder operated by a single camshaft per bank
Bore and stroke: 3.55 in. x 4.16 in.
Displacement: 5.4 liter
Compression ratio: 9.0:1
Induction system: Sequential multi-point fuel injection
Maximum power: 260 bhp at 4,250 rpm
Maximum torque: 330 lb-ft at 3,000 rpm
Top speed: 121 mph
0–60 mph: 8.7 sec.

TRANSMISSION
Four-speed automatic

BODY/CHASSIS
Separate steel chassis with steel pickup body

SPECIAL FEATURES

The Dale Jarret Special Edition features unique rear window graphic...

...as well as a special induction hood and distinctive billet aluminum grill.

RUNNING GEAR
Steering: Recirculating ball
Front suspension: Unequal length A-arms with coil springs, telescopic shock absorbers and anti-roll bar
Rear suspension: Live axle with semi-elliptic multi-leaf springs and telescopic shock absorbers
Brakes: Vented discs (front), drums (rear), ABS
Wheels: ULTRA cast-aluminum, 9 x 17 in.
Tires: Toyo Prox S/T, 285/60 R17

DIMENSIONS
Length: 220.8 in.   **Width:** 78.4 in.
Height: 72.8 in.   **Wheelbase:** 138.5 in.
Track: 65.4 in. (front and rear)
Weight: 4,067 lbs.

Ford **F-350 SUPER DUTY**

Ford's Super Duty series of light- and medium-weight trucks are intimidating enough in stock form, but for some, too much is never enough. Witness this high-riding F-350, which, with its substantial lift, is worthy of being called a junior monster truck.

"...moves along effortlessly."

"As imposing as it looks, this truck rides relatively smoothly even with an 8-inch lift and monster tires, due in part to the custom multistage leaf packs on the front and rear. Four-wheel drive is activated simply by the touch of a button in the cockpit. This lets the monster rig move effortlessly over the most challenging terrain, while protecting its occupants from the extremities of the great outdoors."

SVO leather-trimmed seats give the cabin a luxurious feel, and a CB radio enables contact with the outside world.

Milestones

1996 Ford introduces
a brand-new F-150, which adopts the aero look. It is sold as a 1997 model and production is allocated to three of the five plants used to build F-series trucks. The square-rigged 1996 model continues to be produced until the end of the year.

First of the new wave of F-series trucks was the F-150, the world's best-selling vehicle.

1998 The bigger F-series
trucks are supplanted by an all-new Super Duty series, starting with the F-250 and F-350 formats. The standard engine is the 5.4-liter V8, but a 6.8-liter V10 and Power Stroke diesel are optional.

With the 1999 Super Duty rigs, Ford has redefined the concept of big, workhorse pickups.

1999 The biggest members
of the F-series—the Super Duty F-600 and F-700—go on sale, replacing the previous 1980-vintage models.

UNDER THE SKIN

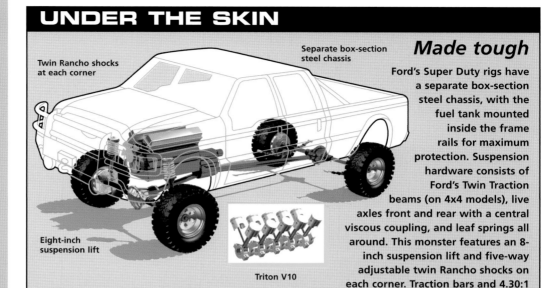

Twin Rancho shocks at each corner

Separate box-section steel chassis

Eight-inch suspension lift

Triton V10

Made tough

Ford's Super Duty rigs have a separate box-section steel chassis, with the fuel tank mounted inside the frame rails for maximum protection. Suspension hardware consists of Ford's Twin Traction beams (on 4x4 models), live axles front and rear with a central viscous coupling, and leaf springs all around. This monster features an 8-inch suspension lift and five-way adjustable twin Rancho shocks on each corner. Traction bars and 4.30:1 gears are among its modifications.

THE POWER PACK

The Power of Ten

Realizing that Dodge had cornered a considerable part of the heavy-duty market with its V10-powered 2500 and 3500 rigs, Ford needed a rival engine. The result is the 412-cubic inch (6.8-liter) Triton V10. It has a cast-iron block and cylinder heads and two valves for each cylinder, but these are actuated by a single overhead camshaft on each bank rather than by a single block camshaft. This means that although the engine still produces masses of torque (410 lb-ft), it does not run out of breath at higher rpm like its rival's engines. For extra smoothness, the V10 employs a counter-rotating balancer shaft.

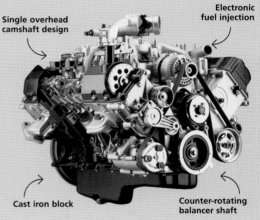

Single overhead camshaft design

Electronic fuel injection

Cast iron block

Counter-rotating balancer shaft

Aiming high

Since they rolled onto the dealers' lots, the new Super Dutys have proved to be popular and are competitively priced. Some owners cannot resist modifying their trucks, and dual exhaust, larger tires, lift kits and extra lights may be fitted.

Oversize tires, bars and winches are popular with the four-wheel drive crowd.

Ford **F-350 SUPER DUTY**

Super Dutys have already found their way into the hands of four-wheeling enthusiasts. This one probably has everything you could possibly need for a long trek into the unforgiving wilds of the Yukon.

Triton V10 engine

In the full-size pickup world, the old adage 'bigger and better' still holds true, especially when it comes to engines. The 6.8-liter V10 is Ford's torquiest production engine of 1999, packing a walloping 410 lb-ft of pulling power.

Twin winches

Off-roading can be hazardous and vehicles can sometimes become stranded. The twin winches on this F-350 (one at the front and one at the rear) can haul loads of up to 12,000 and 9,000 lbs., respectively—far greater weights than the average truck or SUV.

Eight-inch lift

The off-road phenomenon really took off in the 1980s, and there are still a number of people who want to build the ultimate off-road vehicle. This rig has an 8-inch lift kit, which means it can clear all but the biggest rocks when out in the wilderness.

Monster tires

Off-roaders require big, low-pressure tires, which are both durable and grippy. The Dick Cepek F/C radials, measuring a huge 38 x 14.5 x 16.5 inches, are more than adequate for scrambling through rough terrain and suspending the 6,710-lbs. curb weight of the truck. A full-size spare is carried in the pickup bed.

Limiting straps

Although off-roaders require considerable suspension travel in order to clear obstacles, too much can cause problems. For this reason, limiter straps are fitted at the front and rear to prevent the axles from damaging the underside of the vehicle.

Dual shocks

Good damping is essential for four-wheelers, especially when the terrain gets rugged. Dual Rancho shocks at each corner ensure that the driver and passengers are as comfortable as possible when traveling over bumpy ground and that the vehicle remains as stable and as level as possible.

Specifications

1999 Ford F-350 Super Duty

ENGINE

Type: V10

Construction: Cast-iron block and heads

Valve gear: Two valves per cylinder operated by a single overhead camshaft for each cylinder bank

Bore and stroke: 3.55 in. x 4.16 in.

Displacement: 412 c.i.

Compression ratio: 9.0:1

Induction system: Sequential multipoint fuel injection

Maximum power: 275 bhp at 4,250 rpm

Maximum torque: 410 lb-ft at 2,650 rpm

Top speed: 96 mph

0–60 mph: 10.6 sec.

TRANSMISSION

Four-speed automatic

BODY/CHASSIS

Separate steel chassis with four-door pickup body

SPECIAL FEATURES

Due to this truck's substantial step-in height, step plates are essential.

A bed liner helps protect cargo.

RUNNING GEAR

Steering: Recirculating-ball

Front suspension: Twin traction beams with coil springs, quad telescopic shock absorbers and anti-roll bar

Rear suspension: Live axle with coil springs and quad telescopic shock absorbers

Brakes: Discs (front and rear)

Wheels: American Eagle, 16.5 x 12 in.

Tires: Dick Cepek, 38 x 14.5 x 16.5

DIMENSIONS

Length: 265.6 in. **Width:** 104.7 in.

Height: 97.6 in. **Wheelbase:** 156 in.

Track: 86.2 in. (front), 87.6 in. (rear)

Weight: 6,710 lbs.

GMC **STEPSIDE**

Affectionately nicknamed the 'Bullnose,' the FC series appeared halfway through 1947 and ushered in a new era in styling and comfort for light-duty trucks. Today, these vehicles are coveted collectibles.

"...workman-like vehicle."

"Utilitarian is the best way to describe the Stepside. Compared to modern pickups, the interior is spartan, but in its time it was regarded as luxurious. With a straight six under the bulbous hood, this truck is no hot rod but pulls well at low revs, and the floor-mounted gear shifter is quite smooth for such a workman-like vehicle. The ride is quite harsh and bumpy, especially unloaded. Its cornering can be interesting, but all this is part of the Bullnose charm."

The dashboard is dominated by the large speedometer and clock.

Milestones

1947 GMC reveals
a new line of light-duty trucks, with smoother styling and a revamped cab and front suspension. The sole engine is a 228-cubic inch, in-line six, carried over from the old CC/EC series. A total of 49,187 of the new trucks are registered this year.

Chevrolet's version of the GMC FC series is the popular 3100, a straight-six powered pickup.

1950 Power from the six-cylinder
engine increases from 93 to 96 bhp. New shock absorbers help smooth the ride, and improved electricals also arrive.

Chevrolet® (and GMC) trucks were restyled for 1955. This is a 1957 model.

1954 A restyle
results in flashier appearance, and chrome hubcaps and trim return. The six is bored out to 249 inches and a one-piece windshield is fitted.

UNDER THE SKIN

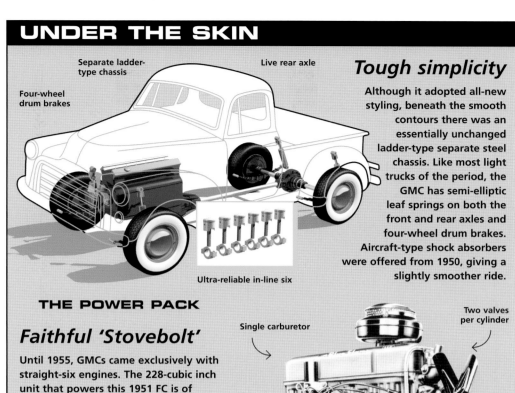

Four-wheel drum brakes

Separate ladder-type chassis

Live rear axle

Ultra-reliable in-line six

Tough simplicity
Although it adopted all-new styling, beneath the smooth contours there was an essentially unchanged ladder-type separate steel chassis. Like most light trucks of the period, the GMC has semi-elliptic leaf springs on both the front and rear axles and four-wheel drum brakes. Aircraft-type shock absorbers were offered from 1950, giving a slightly smoother ride.

THE POWER PACK

Faithful 'Stovebolt'
Until 1955, GMCs came exclusively with straight-six engines. The 228-cubic inch unit that powers this 1951 FC is of Chevrolet origin and dates back to 1927. It is an all-iron, L-head unit with a four-main-bearing crankshaft. Engineered by Ormond E. Hunt, it was affectionately known as the 'Stovebolt Six,' so named because of the engine's cast-iron pistons and slotted head bolts. Outfitted with hydraulic valve lifters and a Carter one-barrel carburetor, it produces 100 bhp at just 3,400 rpm.

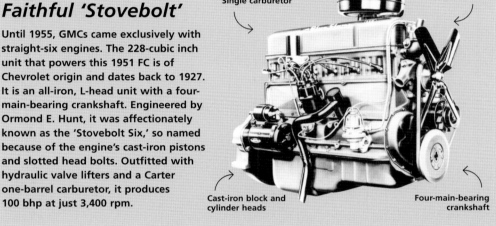

Single carburetor

Two valves per cylinder

Cast-iron block and cylinder heads

Four-main-bearing crankshaft

Big brother
Essentially, the FC series is an upmarket Chevrolet 3100 with virtually identical sheet metal and cab. But the GMC version has a larger, more powerful engine (100-bhp, 228-cubic inch versus 92-bhp, 217-cubic inch). The GMC attracts less collector interest than the Chevrolet, but buyers get more for their money.

Better refined and more powerful post-1950 models are the best buy.

GMC **STEPSIDE**

Smooth styling and improved ergonomics marked GMC's first 'new' post-war pickups. More powerful, better trimmed and more exclusive than rival Chevrolets, they signaled a move toward the leisure market.

Stepside bed
Traditional pickup beds were called 'stepsides' because running boards enabled people to step up into the bed.

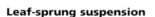

Leaf-sprung suspension
Traditionally, trucks had leaf-sprung suspensions. This setup is simple and rugged and can cope admirably with rough roads, but does not sacrifice too much in the way of ride comfort.

Optional gas tank
Buyers could choose a number of options on their new GMC in 1951. Among them was the position of the gas tank. This is mounted under the pickup bed as standard, although a cab-mounted tank could be ordered instead.

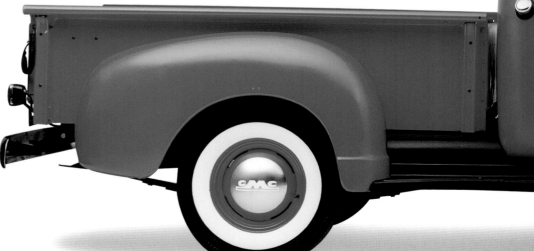

Improved cab

One of the most noticeable differences of the 1947-1955 GMCs was a more spacious cab than earlier CC/EC-series trucks. The headroom was increased by one inch and legroom by seven inches. A larger glass area improved visibility.

Dual shocks

Buyers could order a set of auxiliary shock absorbers at the rear. These were especially welcomed by those who purchased the FC to carry heavy loads.

Optional lights

Back in 1951, twin tail and stop lights were optional. Today, due to the density of traffic, many owners have chosen to fit these items.

Stovebolt Six

One of the most reliable engines ever built, the veteran Chevy six was a mainstay in GMCs until 1955. GMCs had a larger unit as standard than the rival Chevrolet 3100.

Specifications

1951 GMC FC-101 Stepside

ENGINE
Type: In-line six
Construction: Cast-iron block and heads
Valve gear: Two valves per cylinder operated by pushrods and rockers
Bore and stroke: 3.56 in. x 3.81 in.
Displacement: 228 c.i.
Compression ratio: 6.6:1
Induction system: Carter single-barrel carburetor
Maximum power: 100 bhp at 3,400 rpm
Maximum torque: 187 lb-ft at 1,700 rpm
Top speed: 83 mph
0–60 mph: 22.0 sec.

TRANSMISSION
Four-speed manual

BODY/CHASSIS
Steel ladder frame with steel cab and bed

SPECIAL FEATURES

A 100 badge on the side of the hood signifies a 100-bhp 'Stovebolt Six.'

Single circular headlights were fitted to all GMCs up until 1957.

RUNNING GEAR
Steering: Recirculating ball
Front suspension: Solid axle with leaf springs and telescopic shock absorbers
Rear suspension: Live axle with leaf springs and telescopic shock absorbers
Brakes: Drums (front and rear)
Wheels: Pressed steel, 15-in. dia.
Tires: Bias-ply, 6.00 x 16

DIMENSIONS
Length: 196.6 in.   **Width:** 68.0 in.
Height: 67.0 in.   **Wheelbase:** 116.0 in.
Track: 57.6 in. (front), 60.0 in. (rear)
Weight: 3,275 lbs.

GMC SYCLONE

Sports cars are for speed, pickup trucks are for hauling around cargo, right? But what if you could combine the two and build a pickup as fast as a Vette™? No, it's not impossible and GM proved it with 280 bhp of turbocharged V6.

"...pure attitude."

"You've seen custom trucks cruising Saturday nights for years. But you've got one of only 3,000 Syclones ever made and there's nothing like it. With big wheels, spoilers, skirts and an intercooled turbo, this hot-rod truck is pure attitude. Finally, a factory show-and-go truck! Hit the gas and you've got instant acceleration—a thump in the back that sends you rocketing off the line to 30 mph in less than two seconds. OK, it's not a sports car, but for a small pickup, there's surprising handling and comfort."

Sport seats and a leather steering wheel give the Syclone's interior a sports car feel.

Milestones

1970s Japanese manufacturers start to make a real impact in the pickup truck market in the U.S. with smaller, nimbler trucks that are more fun than anything from Ford or GM. Some American manufacturers go so far as to offer Japanese trucks with American badges.

The success of the Japanese mini-trucks pushed U.S. manufacturers to produce faster trucks.

1982 America hits back with small trucks of its own: GMC brings out the S15 sports pickup with a new V6 engine, while Ford, reacting in the same way, improves the Ranger pickup.

1991 Adding a liquid-cooled intercooler to the 4.3-liter V6, GMC produces the limited-edition 280-bhp Syclone. It's General Motors' showcase to prove just what performance you can get from a truck. Only 800 were built during this Syclone's short production run.

Once the Syclone was dropped in 1992, the S10 series lost its performance variant.

UNDER THE SKIN

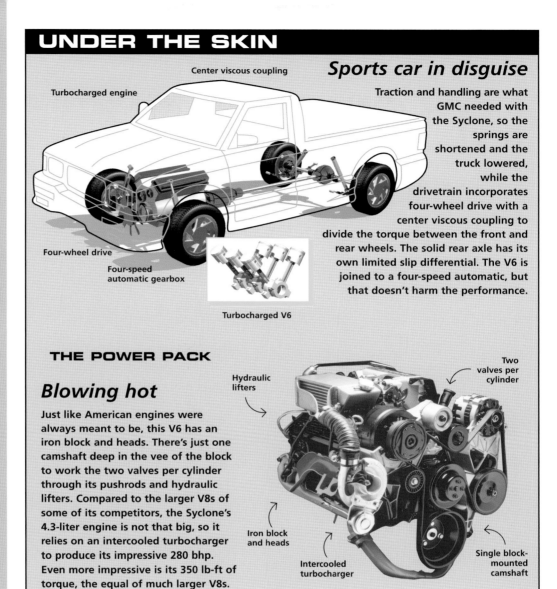

Center viscous coupling

Turbocharged engine

Four-wheel drive

Four-speed automatic gearbox

Turbocharged V6

Sports car in disguise

Traction and handling are what GMC needed with the Syclone, so the springs are shortened and the truck lowered, while the drivetrain incorporates four-wheel drive with a center viscous coupling to divide the torque between the front and rear wheels. The solid rear axle has its own limited slip differential. The V6 is joined to a four-speed automatic, but that doesn't harm the performance.

THE POWER PACK

Blowing hot

Just like American engines were always meant to be, this V6 has an iron block and heads. There's just one camshaft deep in the vee of the block to work the two valves per cylinder through its pushrods and hydraulic lifters. Compared to the larger V8s of some of its competitors, the Syclone's 4.3-liter engine is not that big, so it relies on an intercooled turbocharger to produce its impressive 280 bhp. Even more impressive is its 350 lb-ft of torque, the equal of much larger V8s.

Hydraulic lifters

Two valves per cylinder

Iron block and heads

Intercooled turbocharger

Single block-mounted camshaft

Show and go

GMC gussied up the Syclone so much—with alloy wheels, pointless front spoiler and deep side skirts—you might not take it seriously the first time you come across one. That would be your mistake; from a standstill, this truck can reach 100 mph in less than 18 seconds.

The Syclone is a truck on the outside, sports car on the inside.

GMC **SYCLONE**

When Porsche builds something with an intercooled turbocharger and four-wheel drive, it can cost as much as a house. When GMC did it with the Syclone, you could afford one and have just as much fun while moving the family furniture.

Turbocharged V6

With no room for a big V8 under the hood, GMC opted to turbocharge the existing 4.3-liter V6. That instantly gave more than an extra 120 bhp and in excess of another 100 lb-ft of torque, the ingredient you need for serious acceleration.

Side skirts

To make the Syclone look even lower, add-on skirts bring the body line lower between the wheels. They're cosmetic only—there's no real need to manage the airflow under the truck.

Borla Exhaust

To further exploit power, this Syclone has been modified with a free-flowing Borla cat-back exhaust system.

Liquid intercooler

Turbocharged engines work more efficiently if the air that's being forced in can stay dense and cool. To do that, GM uses an intercooler, essentially a radiator for the intake air, which is liquid cooled rather than the more normal air cooling.

Low-profile tires

Wide, low-profile tires are installed in the Syclone to help traction and road holding. They work well enough to generate 0.8g around the skid pad. Not many pickups can manage that.

Rear drum brakes

Because its front brakes do all the work, the Syclone can get by with drum brakes at the rear working in conjunction with the ABS. Brakes are just as impressive as the acceleration.

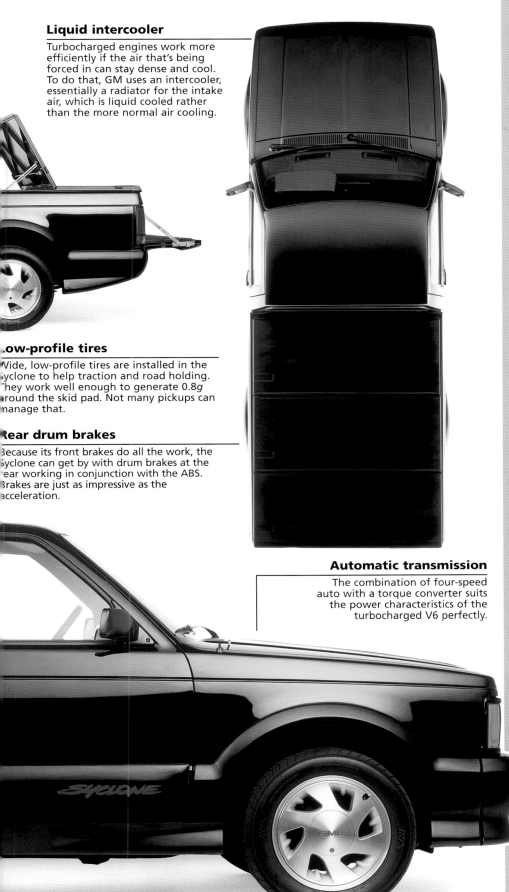

Automatic transmission

The combination of four-speed auto with a torque converter suits the power characteristics of the turbocharged V6 perfectly.

Specifications

1992 GMC Syclone

ENGINE

Type: V6
Construction: Cast-iron block and head
Valve gear: Two valves per cylinder operated by single block-mounted camshaft via pushrods, rockers and hydraulic lifters
Bore and stroke: 4 in. x 3.48 in.
Displacement: 4,293 cc
Compression ratio: 8.35:1
Induction system: Electronic multi-point fuel injection with intercooled turbocharger
Maximum power: 280 bhp at 4,400 rpm
Maximum torque: 350 lb-ft at 3,600 rpm
Top speed: 126 mph
0–60 mph: 4.9 sec.

TRANSMISSION

Four-speed automatic with four-wheel drive and center viscous coupling

BODY/CHASSIS

Steel frame with two-door pickup body

SPECIAL FEATURES

The sporting theme carries on inside the Syclone. Body-hugging bucket seats hold driver and passenger firmly in position under hard cornering.

An intercooled turbocharger helps the V6 give the power of a much larger V8.

RUNNING GEAR

Steering: Recirculating ball
Front suspension: Unequal-length control arms, torsion bars, anti-roll bar and telescopic shock absorbers
Rear suspension: Live axle with semi-elliptic leaf springs and telescopic shocks
Brakes: Discs (front), drums (rear) with ABS
Wheels: Alloy, 8 in. x 16 in.
Tires: Yokohama AVS 245/50 VR16

DIMENSIONS

Length: 180.5 in.   **Width:** 68.2 in.
Height: 60 in.   **Wheelbase:** 108.3 in.
Track: 55.7 in. (front), 54.1 in. (rear)
Weight: 3,599 lbs.

GMC TYPHOON

It's quicker than a Ferrari 348, and has greater luggage capacity. It also boasts all-wheel drive and is powered with a turbocharged engine. However, this vehicle is not an ultra-expensive supercar, but a high performance sport utility from GMC.

"...heart-stopping acceleration."

"With the ride height lowered and the springs and shocks stiffened, you soon realize that you can use as much of the Typhoon's 280 bhp as you like. The all-wheel drive system puts down maximum traction, which results in heart-stopping acceleration with 0–100 mph taking just 16.3 seconds. Cornering ability comes close to matching straight-line performance, while the steering has more than enough feel to inspire confidence."

The Typhoon is like a luxury SUV inside, with leather seats and power everything.

Milestones

1990 GMC turns a Sonoma

pickup truck into the extraordinary Syclone in time for the 1991 model year. It cannot carry a great deal, but it can accelerate to 60 mph faster than a Ferrari 348 or even a Corvette® ZR-1®. It is part of GMC's plan to improve its image.

GM'S other muscle truck at the time was the Chevrolet 454 SS®.

1992 A year after the Syclone,

GMC introduces the Typhoon, which uses the same all-wheel-drive chassis and turbocharged V6 engine combined with a two-door GMC Jimmy® body. Like the Syclone®, the Typhoon is well received by the press and achieves status as the world's fastest SUV.

The Typhoon is based on the popular GMC Jimmy.

1992 The Syclone is dropped,

but the Typhoon continues. Only 2,200 are built and production ends this year.

UNDER THE SKIN

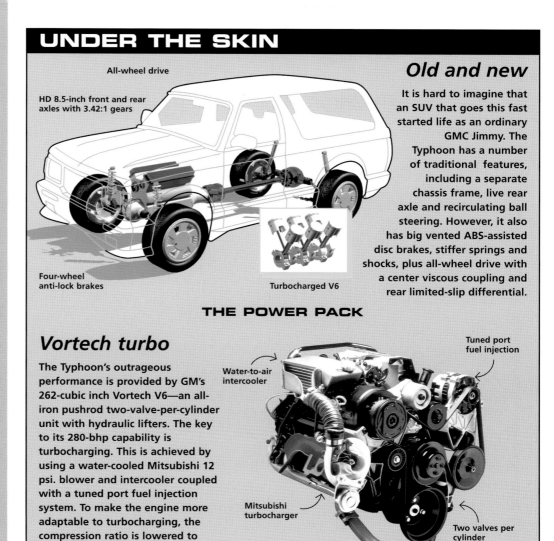

All-wheel drive

HD 8.5-inch front and rear axles with 3.42:1 gears

Four-wheel anti-lock brakes

Turbocharged V6

Old and new

It is hard to imagine that an SUV that goes this fast started life as an ordinary GMC Jimmy. The Typhoon has a number of traditional features, including a separate chassis frame, live rear axle and recirculating ball steering. However, it also has big vented ABS-assisted disc brakes, stiffer springs and shocks, plus all-wheel drive with a center viscous coupling and rear limited-slip differential.

THE POWER PACK

Vortech turbo

The Typhoon's outrageous performance is provided by GM's 262-cubic inch Vortech V6—an all-iron pushrod two-valve-per-cylinder unit with hydraulic lifters. The key to its 280-bhp capability is turbocharging. This is achieved by using a water-cooled Mitsubishi 12 psi. blower and intercooler coupled with a tuned port fuel injection system. To make the engine more adaptable to turbocharging, the compression ratio is lowered to 8.4:1 by flat-top pistons.

Water-to-air intercooler

Tuned port fuel injection

Mitsubishi turbocharger

Two valves per cylinder

Whirlwind

Sharing the same running gear as the Typhoon but with a Sonoma pickup truck body, the Syclone has an even more savage character. When it appeared in 1991 its 0–60 mph time of 4.9 seconds made it one of the quickest production vehicles on sale in the U.S.

A unique drivetrain and low production ensures future collectability.

GMC TYPHOON

Many Sports Utility Vehicles (SUVs) are misnamed. Most of them do not have nearly enough power to provide real sport performance. The Typhoon is different; it combines sport and utility like no other vehicle.

V6 engine

In the ordinary GMC Jimmy the all-iron overhead-valve V6 engine gives just 165 bhp. In the Typhoon this is raised to an astonishing 280 bhp by turbocharging, intercooling and recalibrating the electronic engine control.

Viscous coupling

To split the torque 35:65 front/rear a mechanical center differential is fitted in series with a viscous coupling. The system was first seen on GMC's all-wheel drive Safari van.

Live axle

At the rear, the Typhoon retains a live axle because an independent unit just wouldn't be able to handle the torque from the turbocharged Vortech V6 engine. Both differentials use 3.42 gears.

Four-speed automatic

Unlike standard Jimmys, the Typhoon is fitted with high performance 700 R4 four-speed automatic transmission, as found on many other GM performance vehicles.

Front air dam

Partly to set it aside from the ordinary Jimmy and partly to prevent air from collecting under the vehicle where it could unsettle at speed, a front air dam, complete with fog lights, was added.

Limited-slip differential

Although only 65 percent of the drive goes to the rear wheels through the all-wheel drive system, it is still a great deal of torque. This means a limited-slip differential is required to maintain traction on both rear wheels.

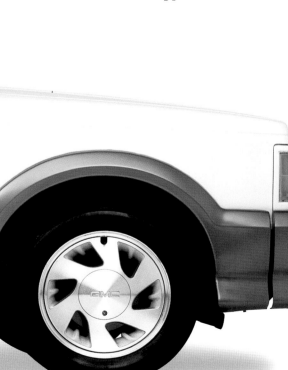

Specifications

1992 GMC Typhoon

ENGINE

Type: V6

Construction: Cast-iron block and heads

Valve gear: Two valves per cylinder operated by pushrods and rockers

Bore and stroke: 4.0 in x 3.5 in

Displacement: 262 c.i.

Compression ratio: 8.4:1

Induction system: Electronic fuel injection with intercooled Mitsubishi RH06 turbocharger

Maximum power: 280 bhp at 4,400 rpm

Maximum torque: 350 lb-ft at 3,600 rpm

Top speed: 124 mph

0–60 mph: 5.4 sec.

TRANSMISSION

GM 700 R4 four-speed automatic

BODY/CHASSIS

Separate steel frame with steel two-door SUV body

SPECIAL FEATURES

Typhoons have these special Turbine-style wheels as standard equipment.

> **NOTICE**
> DO NOT TOW A TRAILER WITH THIS VEHICLE.
> TOWING CAN CAUSE SEVERE DAMAGE TO ENGINE AND TRANSMISSION.
> THE POWERTRAIN IS NOT DESIGNED FOR TRAILER TOWING.
> PRINTED IN USA   PAS 55897

GMC warns owners not to use the Typhoon for towing.

RUNNING GEAR

Steering: Recirculating ball

Front suspension: Double wishbones with torsion bars, telescopic shock absorbers and anti-roll bar

Rear suspension: Live axle with semi-elliptic leaf springs, telescopic shock absorbers and automatic self-levelling

Brakes: Vented discs, 11.9-in. dia. (front), drums, 11.2-in. dia. (rear)

Wheels: Alloy, 8 x 16 in.

Tires: Firestone Firehawk SVX 245/50 VR16

DIMENSIONS

Length: 170.3 in.   **Width:** 68.2 in.

Height: 60.0 in.   **Wheelbase:** 100.5 in.

Track: 57.8 in. (front), 58.0 in. (rear)

Weight: 3,822 lbs.

Isuzu **VEHI-CROSS**

There are some pretty strange-looking vehicles on the road today, but none can compete with the completely bizarre Isuzu Vehi-CROSS. It looks like a concept car but is in fact a regular production model.

"...sports off-roader."

"Although you have to climb up to get into the cabin of the Vehi-CROSS, it feels like you're in a sports car once you're inside. The steering wheel is small and the seats are more like racing buckets.The biggest shock, though, comes when you slot the gear selector into reverse. A warning buzzer sounds and the screen for the satellite navigation switches to a camera mounted on the tailgate. The ride is harsh, but body roll is well controlled for an off-roader."

The Isuzu's interior is more like that of a sports car than an off-roader.

Milestones

1983 Isuzu builds
the first Trooper. It uses a four-cylinder engine and is rather crude in comparison with other 'civilized' off-roaders.

1992 The Trooper is revised
and fitted with a 3.2-liter, 24-valve V6 engine, producing 174 bhp.

Vehi-CROSS rides the short-wheelbase Trooper Citation chassis.

1993 Isuzu shows
the Vehi-CROSS concept car at the Tokyo Motor Show. It is designed by Englishman Simon Cox.

Another stunning new 4x4 Isuzu is the Deseo concept car.

1997 The Vehi-CROSS enters
production. It goes on sale in Japan only.

1998 Isuzu sends test cars around
the world to test the water for sales in the U.S. and other countries.

UNDER THE SKIN

Trooper-based

Despite its moon-buggy-like appearance, the Vehi-CROSS is based on the short-wheelbase Isuzu Trooper chassis. That means double wishbones with longitudinal torsion bars up front and a live rear axle with coil springs. Braking is by four-wheel vented discs. In normal driving conditions the Vehi-CROSS runs 100 percent rear-wheel drive, but when wheel slip is detected the torque being fed to each axle is altered to counteract this.

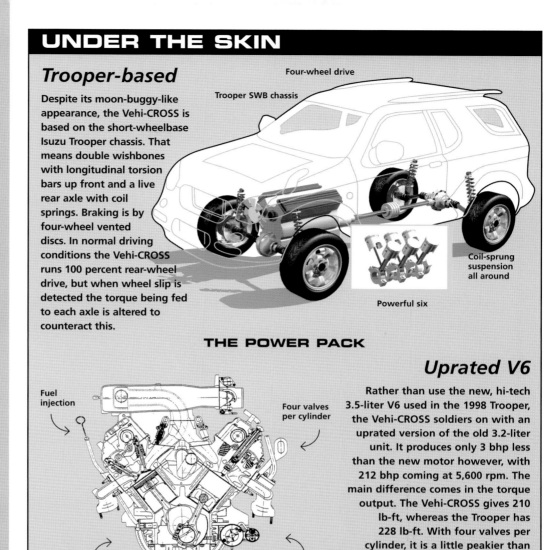

Four-wheel drive

Trooper SWB chassis

Coil-sprung suspension all around

Powerful six

THE POWER PACK

Fuel injection

Four valves per cylinder

Cast-iron block

Alloy cylinder heads

Uprated V6

Rather than use the new, hi-tech 3.5-liter V6 used in the 1998 Trooper, the Vehi-CROSS soldiers on with an uprated version of the old 3.2-liter unit. It produces only 3 bhp less than the new motor however, with 212 bhp coming at 5,600 rpm. The main difference comes in the torque output. The Vehi-CROSS gives 210 lb-ft, whereas the Trooper has 228 lb-ft. With four valves per cylinder, it is a little peakier than some other off-roaders, pushing the Vehi-CROSS towards the top of the 4x4 performance league.

Wacky looks

Given its wacky looks and limited production, the Vehi-CROSS is already a popular niche car. In Japan, buyers are lining up to get their hands on one. There is nothing else like it on the road. In a Vehi-CROSS you are bound to turn heads.

The Vehi-CROSS is certainly unique. Too bad it's not available in the U.S.

Isuzu **VEHI-CROSS**

An award-winning design, the Isuzu Vehi-CROSS is one of those few concept cars that actually made it into production. It looks stunning, outperforms almost all other off-roaders and is built in limited numbers.

Rear-view camera

The Vehi-CROSS' techno-design is reinforced by a special rear-mounted video camera which sends pictures to a 5-inch television screen on the fascia. The video display also has an audio system, which includes a graphic equalizer and an optional satellite navigation system.

Concept car styling

The Vehi-CROSS was originally designed as a concept car and has reached production with few changes.

Sporty interior

Unusually for a big 4x4, the Vehi-CROSS has a rather sporting interior. It has Recaro bucket seats and a small, leather-trimmed Momo steering wheel. For tight parking, the door mirrors fold in at the touch of a button. An extra convex mirror on the front of the fender gives a wider rear view.

Trooper-based running gear

The Vehi-CROSS is based on the Isuzu Trooper. It shares the same wheelbase, suspension and chassis. With its lighter body it has a slightly improved power-to-weight ratio.

'Torque-on-demand'

The new advanced 'Torque-on-demand' four-wheel drive system senses road conditions and adjusts the torque being fed to each axle.

Specifications

1998 Isuzu Vehi-CROSS

ENGINE

Type: V6

Construction: Cast-iron block and alloy cylinder heads

Valve gear: Four valves per cylinder operated by twin overhead camshafts per cylinder bank

Bore and stroke: 3.68 in. x 3.03 in.

Displacement: 3,165 cc

Compression ratio: 9.3:1

Induction system: Fuel injection

Maximum power: 212 bhp at 5,600 rpm

Maximum torque: 210 lb-ft at 3,000 rpm

Top speed: 110 mph

0–60 mph: 9.8 sec.

TRANSMISSION

Four-speed automatic

BODY/CHASSIS

Steel chassis with steel/polypropylene two-door SUV body

SPECIAL FEATURES

The light covers sweep right back into the hood and also incorporate the turn signals.

Wide five-spoke alloy wheels are a standard fitting on the Vehi-CROSS.

RUNNING GEAR

Steering: Recirculating ball

Front suspension: Double wishbones with torsion bars, telescopic aluminum shock absorbers with 'piggy-back' reservoirs and anti-roll bar

Rear suspension: Live axle with coil springs, telescopic aluminum shock absorbers with 'piggy-back' reservoirs and anti-roll bar

Brakes: Vented discs (front and rear); ABS

Wheels: Alloy, 5 x 16 in.

Tires: 245/70 R16

DIMENSIONS

Length: 162.6 in.   **Width:** 70.5 in.

Height: 72.2 in.   **Wheelbase:** 91.7 in.

Track: 59.6 in. (front), 59.8 in. (rear)

Weight: 3,858 lbs.

JAPAN 1998–PRESENT

Isuzu **TROOPER**

Isuzu may be a minnow in Japanese manufacturing terms but it is a giant in the 4x4 sport utility world. The current Trooper is the ultimate expression of Isuzu's expertise in this field.

"...competent and compliant."

"With its wide-track, independent front suspension and coil-sprung rear, the Trooper is more competent on-road than many so-called sport utilities and its steering provides better response. Thick anti-roll bars also enable sharp bends to be tackled with ease. Off-road however, the Trooper really shines. The 3.5-liter V6 is willing, and minimal overhangs enable steep entry and departure angles. Traction is excellent thanks to precise wheel control."

Although more luxurious, the current Trooper is still workmanlike inside.

Milestones

1983 Isuzu launches

its first Trooper on export markets. Initially, it comes standard with a 2.2-liter diesel engine and proves highly popular and reliable.

When the Trooper was launched it went on sale in two- and four-door versions.

1992 A new, revised

Trooper model goes on sale. It is larger and roomier than the previous model and is available with a larger 3.2-liter engine and a five-speed and automatic transmissions. The limited edition SE model joins the lineup for 1994.

Priced below the Trooper is the Rodeo, sold as the Opel/Vauxhall Frontera in European markets.

1998 Isuzu introduces another

Trooper model, which is heavily revised. The line up includes both short and long wheelbases, 3.0 diesel and 3.5 gasoline engines and three different trim levels (Standard, Duty and Citation).

UNDER THE SKIN

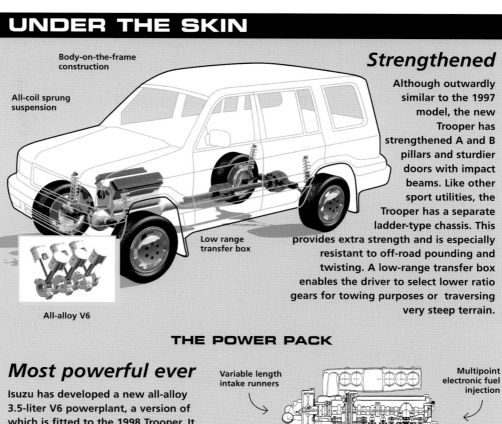

Body-on-the-frame construction

All-coil sprung suspension

Low range transfer box

All-alloy V6

Strengthened

Although outwardly similar to the 1997 model, the new Trooper has strengthened A and B pillars and sturdier doors with impact beams. Like other sport utilities, the Trooper has a separate ladder-type chassis. This provides extra strength and is especially resistant to off-road pounding and twisting. A low-range transfer box enables the driver to select lower ratio gears for towing purposes or traversing very steep terrain.

THE POWER PACK

Most powerful ever

Isuzu has developed a new all-alloy 3.5-liter V6 powerplant, a version of which is fitted to the 1998 Trooper. It has direct ignition with one coil for each spark plug, multipoint fuel injection and four overhead camshafts. The computer-controlled variable intake system optimizes torque and power which peak at 215 bhp at 5,400 rpm and 228 lb-ft at 3,000 rpm respectively. The torquey engine provides more than ample power to move the 4,387 lb. Trooper both on and off the pavement.

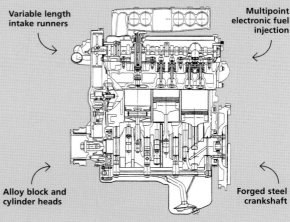

Variable length intake runners

Multipoint electronic fuel injection

Alloy block and cylinder heads

Forged steel crankshaft

Citation 3.5L

The top model in the Trooper range is the 3.5-liter V6 powered Citation. The torquey V6 engine is the most powerful yet fitted to a Trooper, and the Citation offers almost sports car levels of performance and limousine levels of space and comfort.

The Citation combines car-like luxury with rugged off-road ability.

Isuzu **TROOPER**

For years the Trooper has been regarded as the benchmark sport utility in many parts of the world. The latest version further improves on the Trooper's off-road ability, while offering greater luxury and refinement.

Advanced engine

The 3.5-liter V6 gasoline engine is one of the most advanced used in a sport utility vehicle. The 9.4:1 compression engine has four valves per cylinder operated by dual overhead camshafts.

Rugged suspension

A big feature of the Trooper since the beginning has been its tough suspension. An independent wishbone setup is employed at the front, with a coil-sprung live axle at the rear. Thick sway bars help reduce body roll.

Minimal overhangs

The Trooper's off-road ability is helped by very short front and rear overhangs, ensuring approach and departure angles of 31 degrees and 27 degrees respectively. It has a ground clearance of 8.2 inches.

Restrained styling

Although the 1998 Trooper has all new exterior panels, it looks much like its predecessor. The front end is noticeably different with a sloping grill and more rounded fenders.

'Shift-on-the-fly' drive selection

Like many sport utilities and some 4WD cars the Trooper employs a Shift-on-the-fly 4WD system. The driver can select four-wheel drive when needed, and at speeds up to 62 mph. This results in improved fuel economy and also eliminates unnecessary driveline friction.

114

Huge interior space

The LWB Trooper comes with seating for five as standard, including a split/fold rear seat, but you can order a third row of seats. With the rear seats folded, the cabin boasts a cavernous capacity of 85 cubic feet.

Specifications

1998 Isuzu Trooper 3.5 LWB

ENGINE

Type: V6

Construction: Aluminum cylinder block and heads

Valve gear: Four valves per cylinder operated by double overhead camshafts per bank

Bore and stroke: 3.68 in. x 3.35 in.

Displacement: 3,494 cc

Compression ratio: 9.4:1

Induction system: Sequential multipoint fuel injection

Maximum power: 215 bhp at 5,400 rpm

Maximum torque: 228 lb-ft at 3,000 rpm

Top speed: 112 mph

0–60 mph: 9.4 sec.

TRANSMISSION

Five-speed manual or four-speed automatic

BODY/CHASSIS

Separate chassis with five-door sport utility body in steel

SPECIAL FEATURES

A giant hood scoop provides cool air for the intercooler on diesel models.

High ground clearance is essential for traversing rough terrain.

RUNNING GEAR

Steering: Recirculating ball

Front suspension: Double wishbones with torsion bars, shock absorbers and anti-roll bar

Rear suspension: Live axle with coil springs, shock absorbers and anti-roll bar

Brakes: Vented discs (front and rear)

Wheels: Alloy 16-in. dia.

Tires: 245/70 R16

DIMENSIONS

Length: 187.4 in.   **Width:** 72.2 in.

Height: 72.4 in.   **Wheelbase:** 108.6 in.

Track: 59.6 in. (front), 59.8 in. (rear)

Weight: 4,387 lbs.

Jeep **CJ-7**

Building on the legendary reputation of the Jeep name, the CJ-7 added flair and creature comforts to the basic durability for which Jeep was so well known. It was a massive sales hit.

"...unrivaled durability."

"When you've got the proven military record of the post-war Jeeps to build on, you already have the makings of a stunning recreational off-roader. The standard 232-cubic inch six-cylinder engine comfortably pulls the CJ-7 up all but the steepest hills—for which the V8 is needed—and the Jeep's durability is unrivaled among its peers. On-road, the CJ's responsive steering gives surprisingly capable handling, and there's a pliant ride, too."

The CJ-7 addresses passenger comfort with improved legroom and supportive seating.

Milestones

1976 After the success of the Jeep CJ-5, AMC responds to the growth of the leisure industry with the CJ-7, which has a longer wheelbase and six-cylinder power. It is also the first Jeep available with both TurboHydramatic and full-time Quadra-Trac 4WD. Hard-top and soft-top versions are available.

The original Jeep shows how little the design has changed in the transition to a leisure vehicle.

1978 The growth in Jeep sales prompts AMC to turn its Brampton, Ontario, plant over to Jeep production exclusively. The special-edition 'Golden Eagle' goes on sale.

The modern Wrangler Sport keeps the Jeep tradition alive.

1984 A new 2.5-liter engine is introduced, while the 'Limited' CJ-7 is discontinued.

1986 After 10 years of production, the last '7' is made.

UNDER THE SKIN

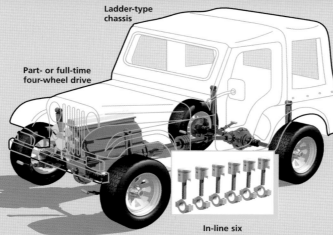

Ladder-type chassis

Part- or full-time four-wheel drive

In-line six

THE POWER PACK

Classic evolution

At the heart of the Jeep's rugged construction is a standard ladder-type frame—little changed from versions of the Jeep used in World War II. The suspension is by semi-elliptic leaf springs on a live axle with tube shocks. The standard transmission is a three-speed manual, with part-time four-wheel drive with a Dana 20 transfer case. The real change was that 'Quadra-Trac' four-wheel drive was optional on the automatic version.

Tough torquing

No-nonsense off-road utility vehicles need strong, reliable engines, and the Jeep is no exception. Although three engines were offered—two in-line sixes and a V8—the standard powerplant was AMC's torquey 232-cubic inch 100 bhp engine. Emissions regulations in California meant that models sold there used the 258-cubic inch single-barrel carburetor version of the engine, which was cleaner but had the same power output. The popular Renegade model has a 304-cubic inch V8 with 110 bhp.

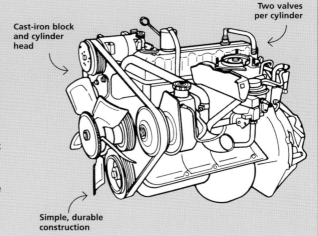

Two valves per cylinder

Cast-iron block and cylinder head

Simple, durable construction

Top of the line

Offered from 1980, the Laredo was a top-line trim package on the CJ-5 and CJ-7. It included 8x15-inch chrome plated wheels with center caps, Goodyear Wrangler 9R tires, chromed front and rear bumpers, hood latch and mirrors, plus an uprated interior with high-back front bucket seats and a leather- rimmed steering wheel.

Laredo models tapped into the growing 4x4 luxury market.

Jeep CJ-7 🇺🇸

While most of the U.S. car market faced a depression in the mid-1970s, AMC's Jeep witnessed a positive boom, thanks in part to the many available variations.

Soft- or hard-top

A soft-top had been used on Jeeps since the post-war years. The CJ-7 broke new ground when it became the first Jeep to offer a polycarbonate removable hard-top attachment. It included metal doors and roll-down windows.

Engine options

Although a V8 and large-capacity in-line six were also available, the standard, 232-cubic inch AMC in-line six is torquey enough to deal with all but the worst off-road conditions.

Renegade models

One of a number of variations on the standard CJ-7, the sporty Renegade model shown here includes a 'swing-away' spare tire attachment as standard equipment as well as other interior creature comforts.

Roll-bar design

By the time the CJ-7 arrived, the central roll-bar structure had become a permanent fixture on the Jeep. Roll bar padding was offered as an accessory from 1981.

Consistent identity

Although the Jeep has appeared in many different styles and finishes, the basic body shape and distinctive grill design have remained unchanged since World War II. The CJ-7 marked major under-the-skin changes, but nothing altered the vehicle's essential character.

Four-wheel drive options

Standard manual CJ-7s use a part-time four-wheel drive system, while automatic models used the 'Quadra-Trac' permanent arrangement.

Specifications

1977 Jeep CJ-7

ENGINE

Type: In-line six-cylinder

Construction: Cast-iron block and head

Valve gear: Two valves per cylinder operated by a single camshaft with pushrods and rockers

Bore and stroke: 3.75 in. x 3.50 in.

Displacement: 232 c.i.

Compression ratio: 8.0:1

Induction system: Single two-barrel carburetor

Maximum power: 100 bhp at 3,600 rpm

Maximum torque: 185 lb-ft at 1,800 rpm

Top speed: 73 mph

0–60 mph: 11.4 sec.

TRANSMISSION

Three-speed manual

BODY/CHASSIS

Ladder-type frame chassis with steel body

SPECIAL FEATURES

The hood attachment levers are unique and, like everything else, built to last.

A fold-down windshield was optional on later CJ-7s.

RUNNING GEAR

Steering: Recirculating ball

Front suspension: Live axle with semi-elliptic leaf springs and tube shock absorbers

Rear suspension: Live axle with semi-elliptic leaf springs and tube shock absorbers

Brakes: Discs, 12-in. dia. (front), drums, 11 x 2-in. (rear)

Wheels: Steel, 6 x 15 in.

Tires: Tracker A/T, 9 x 15 in.

DIMENSIONS

Length: 147.9 in.   **Width:** 65.3 in.

Height: 67.6 in.   **Wheelbase:** 93.5 in.

Track: 54.0 in. (front), 52.5 in. (rear)

Weight: 3,100 lbs.

119

Jeep CHEROKEE

In the mid-1980s, a brand-new Jeep made its debut. It boasted up-to-the-minute styling, a large interior and exceptional go-anywhere ability. It was also the first four-door compact SUV (sport utility vehicle).

"...goes where others cannot."

"Although it is one of the oldest SUVs on the market, the Cherokee is still one of the best. The interior is basic but more practical than many rivals, and cargo space is plentiful. The 190-bhp in-line six launches the Cherokee to 60 mph in a very respectable 8.3 seconds. Handling is good too, and it corners nearly as well as a normal car. Better still, off-road prowess is exceptional, and the Jeep can still go places where larger trucks cannot."

In 1997, the Cherokee got a completely revised interior with twin airbags.

Milestones

1984 A brand-new series of XJ sport utilities makes its debut. Offered as the Cherokee and Wagoneer, in two- or four-door forms, they prove popular. Powerplants are a 2.5-liter four-cylinder or a 2.8-liter V6.

The previous Cherokee was much larger, with optional V8 power. It is more utilitarian than luxurious.

1987 A 4.0-liter 'Power-Tech' six replaces the small V6 engine.

1988 Chrysler takes over AMC and begins upscaling the Jeep line.

The Cherokee's bigger brother is the Grand Cherokee. It was introduced in 1993.

1993 Cherokee sales begin to skyrocket due to its more upscaled styling.

1997 The Cherokee gets an improved interior, a stiffer chassis and a new body with slightly smoother contours.

UNDER THE SKIN

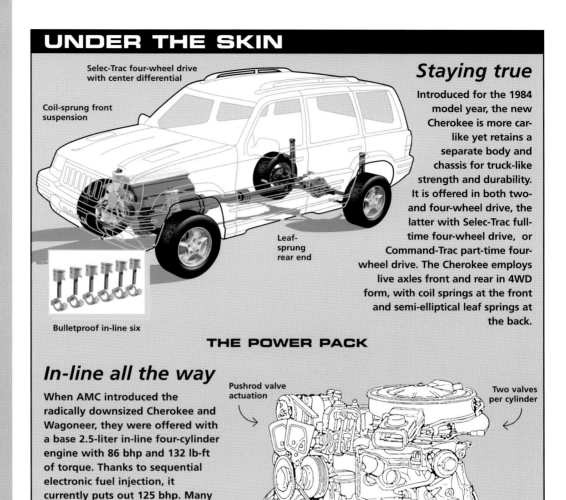

Selec-Trac four-wheel drive with center differential

Coil-sprung front suspension

Leaf-sprung rear end

Bulletproof in-line six

Staying true

Introduced for the 1984 model year, the new Cherokee is more car-like yet retains a separate body and chassis for truck-like strength and durability. It is offered in both two- and four-wheel drive, the latter with Selec-Trac full-time four-wheel drive, or Command-Trac part-time four-wheel drive. The Cherokee employs live axles front and rear in 4WD form, with coil springs at the front and semi-elliptical leaf springs at the back.

THE POWER PACK

In-line all the way

When AMC introduced the radically downsized Cherokee and Wagoneer, they were offered with a base 2.5-liter in-line four-cylinder engine with 86 bhp and 132 lb-ft of torque. Thanks to sequential electronic fuel injection, it currently puts out 125 bhp. Many buyers, however, upgrade to the 4.0-liter 'Power-Tech' six. This bulletproof engine is ideal for off-road excursions and towing heavy loads due, in part, to its 225 lb-ft of torque.

Pushrod valve actuation

Two valves per cylinder

Hydraulic roller lifters

Cast-iron block and cylinder head

Sportiest yet

Without a doubt, the current Cherokee is the best so far, yet it retains the go-anywhere ability of its predecessor. For the most fun, utility and value, the best choice is probably a 4.0-liter Sport model in either two- or four-door form.

The Sport model is probably the best buy.

Jeep **CHEROKEE**

The first compact SUV to offer four doors, the Cherokee is still hugely popular today despite fierce competition. This is due to a sound basic design that offers considerable value for money.

Major makeo

Rattles, squeaks and excessive wind n
have been greatly reduced thanks
stiffer and more aerodynamic b

Choice of transmissions

A five-speed manual, and three- or four-speed automatic transmission is offered with both the 2.5- and 4.0-liter engines.

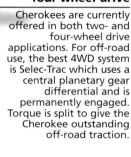

Selec-Trac four-wheel drive

Cherokees are currently offered in both two- and four-wheel drive applications. For off-road use, the best 4WD system is Selec-Trac which uses a central planetary gear differential and is permanently engaged. Torque is split to give the Cherokee outstanding off-road traction.

Coil-sprung front suspension

Even in four-wheel drive form, the Cherokee retains front coil springs, although leaf springs are fitted at the rear. Combined with anti-roll bars front and rear, the Cherokee has car-like handling.

Dual airbags

The vast majority of new vehicles currently on sale in the U.S. have supplementary restraint systems. In 1995 Cherokees were equipped with a driver-side airbag. When the interior was completely revised for 1997, a passenger airbag also became an option. Other safety items include seat belt pre-tensioners and steel beams in the doors.

Boxy styling

When first introduced, the Cherokee boasted up-to-the-minute looks. Its style has become boxier with time, yet its appeal remains undiminished.

'Power-Tech' engine

The majority of buyers specify the straight-six engine. With 190 bhp, it is one of the fastest compact SUVs on sale.

Specifications

1998 Jeep Cherokee 4.0 Limited

ENGINE

Type: In-line six-cylinder

Construction: Cast-iron block and head

Valve gear: Two valves per cylinder operated by a single camshaft with pushrods and rockers

Bore and stroke: 3.88 in. x 3.41 in.

Displacement: 242 c.i.

Compression ratio: 8.8:1

Induction system: Sequential multipoint electronic fuel injection

Maximum power: 190 bhp at 4,600 rpm

Maximum torque: 225 lb-ft at 3,000 rpm

Top speed: 118 mph

0–60 mph: 8.3 sec.

TRANSMISSION

Four-speed automatic

BODY/CHASSIS

Steel ladder-type chassis with separate steel four-door body

SPECIAL FEATURES

Like the original Willys-Overland Jeeps, the Cherokee is built in Toledo, Ohio.

A lighter yet stronger tailgate makes getting heavy items in and out of the back much easier.

RUNNING GEAR

Steering: Recirculating ball

Front suspension: Live axle with coil springs, telescopic shock absorbers and anti-roll bar

Rear suspension: Live axle with semi-elliptic leaf springs, telescopic shock absorbers and anti-roll bar

Brakes: Vented discs (front), drums (rear)

Wheels: Steel, 7.0 x 15 in.

Tires: Goodyear Wrangler, 225/75 SR15

DIMENSIONS

Length: 167.5 in. **Width:** 69.4 in.

Height: 64.0 in. **Wheelbase:** 101.4 in.

Track: 58.0 in. (front and rear)

Weight: 3,360 lbs.

Jeep **GRAND CHEROKEE**

Capitalizing on the past success of the Jeep name and heritage, Chrysler launched the Grand Cherokee for 1993. It's a large, luxurious, all-purpose machine and is capable of the sort of high performance normally reserved for sports cars.

"...an off-road sports car."

"Equipped with a V8 engine, the Grand Cherokee can take on all comers with the acceleration to rival sports cars. Furthermore, it does not roll through corners like most off-roaders. Ride quality is also good, even in rough conditions, and the sophisticated 4x4 system makes light work of difficult terrain. Inside, the Grand Cherokee Limited is fully equipped, better than many luxury cars on the market."

The Grand Cherokee has full instrumentation and features such luxuries as power seats and climate control.

Milestones

1992 Chrysler boss Bob Lutz reveals the
Grand Cherokee by driving the first one from the factory, along the streets of Detroit and through a plate-glass window at the Detroit Auto Show.

The Wrangler is currently the entry-level vehicle and the most traditional in the Jeep range.

1994 European production begins at
Chrysler's plant in Graz, Austria.

1996 The 1,000,000th Grand Cherokee rolls off the
assembly line.

Since 1984 the Cherokee has remained a consistent winner in terms of sales.

1997 The new Grand Cherokee 5.9
Limited, equipped with a larger, 360-cubic inch V8, makes its debut to American buyers.

UNDER THE SKIN

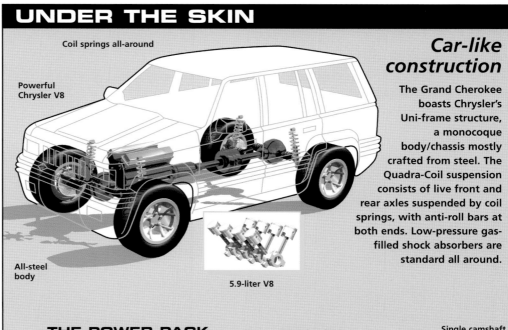

Coil springs all-around

Powerful Chrysler V8

All-steel body

5.9-liter V8

Car-like construction

The Grand Cherokee boasts Chrysler's Uni-frame structure, a monocoque body/chassis mostly crafted from steel. The Quadra-Coil suspension consists of live front and rear axles suspended by coil springs, with anti-roll bars at both ends. Low-pressure gas-filled shock absorbers are standard all around.

THE POWER PACK

Awesome pulling power

While the Grand Cherokee is available with a six-cylinder engine and smaller V8, the Limited LX has the throaty growl of a 360-cubic inch V8, which dates from the 1960s. This engine also powers the mid-size Dodge Dakota, Durango sport-utility vehicle, and the full-size Ram pick-up. In the Limited, it produces 237 bhp and a huge 345 lb-ft of torque. This large engine enables the Grand Cherokee Limited LX to pull a trailer of up to 5,000 lbs.

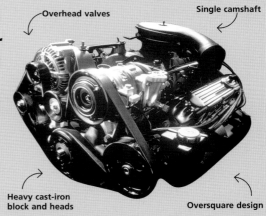

Overhead valves

Single camshaft

Heavy cast-iron block and heads

Oversquare design

Limited LX

Launched in September 1997, the 5.9 Limited is the current flagship. The fastest Jeep ever marketed, it is also exceedingly capable off road and has one of the most luxurious and well-equipped interiors of any sport-utility vehicle. It may not be for everyone, but the 5.9 Limited is one of the best 4x4s in the world.

Enduring style is part of the Grand Cherokee's popularity.

Jeep GRAND CHEROKEE

Taking up its position at the top of the Chrysler Jeep tree, the 5.9 Limited provides the performance of a sports car, the luxury of a limousine, and the off-road ability of a Jeep.

Big V8 engine

The 360-cubic inch V8 runs smooth and provides ample torque. Sophisticated fuel injection and tough cast-iron construction, make for a reliable and robust powerplant.

Aerodynamic des

Compared to contem-porary cars, a drag coefficient figure of 0.45 seems quite hi The Grand Cherokee, however, is one of th most aerodynamic spc utility vehicles ever bu thanks to its raked fro windshield and relativ low roof line.

Built-in roof rack

The sleek, contoured built-in roof rack increases the already-large luggage capacity.

Quadra-Trac four-wheel drive

An on-demand 4x4 system uses a viscous coupling center differential to split the torque between front and rear axles depending on ground surface conditions.

Steep approach angle

With its small front overhang, the Grand Cherokee has an approach angle up hills of 37 degrees and a departure angle of 30 degrees.

Specifications
1998 Jeep Grand Cherokee Limited LX

ENGINE
Type: V8

Construction: Cast-iron block and heads

Valve gear: Two overhead valves per cylinder with hydraulic lifters

Bore and stroke: 4.02 in. x 3.58 in.

Displacement: 360 c.i.

Compression ratio: 8.7:1

Induction system: Fuel injection

Maximum power: 245 bhp at 4,050 rpm

Maximum torque: 345 lb-ft at 3,050 rpm

Top speed: 124 mph

0–60 mph: 8.2 sec.

TRANSMISSION
Four-speed automatic

BODY/CHASSIS
Steel monocoque five-door sport-utility

SPECIAL FEATURES

It's a tight squeeze under the hood, but the 360-cubic inch V8 engine gives outstanding performance.

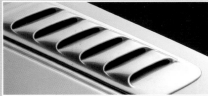

Hood vents distinguish the 5.9 Limited from lesser models.

RUNNING GEAR
Steering: Power-assisted recirculating ball

Front suspension: Live axle suspended by coil springs with leading arms, shocks, and anti-roll bar

Rear suspension: Live axle suspended by coil springs with trailing arms, shocks, and anti-roll bar

Brakes: Vented discs front and rear, anti-lock brake system

Wheels: Alloy, 16-in. dia.

Tires: 225/70 R16

DIMENSIONS
Length: 177.2 in.   **Width:** 70.7 in.

Height: 64.9 in.   **Wheelbase:** 105.9 in.

Track: 58.5 in. (front), 58.8 in. (rear)

Weight: 4,218 lbs.

Jeep WRANGLER

Almost a million Jeeps were built during World War II. They were simple, rugged, reliable and could go almost anywhere. It is these qualities that customers look for in the current Wrangler, introduced in 1997.

"...original off-roader"

"What began as the original purpose-built military off-roader is still built today, but is used more as a trendy transporter than the capable four-wheeler that it is. The Jeep is a fun and very capable off-road vehicle, where its short wheel-base is an asset and the suspension gives more wheel travel and better approach and departure angles. This means the Jeep's abilities are now better than ever. Acceleration and refinement are also notably improved."

The interior of the latest Wrangler is much more comfortable than that of the old model.

Milestones

1987 A new Jeep,

called the Wrangler, replaces the long-running CJ series. The latest model features a restyled body with square headlights, an improved interior and smoother ride, but it retains the go-anywhere capability.

Current Wranglers still bear a resemblance to the original Jeep.

1991 Having bought

American Motors in 1988, Chrysler introduces a performance Wrangler known as the Renegade, with wider body extensions and a 4.0-liter six-cylinder engine.

The forerunner of the Wrangler was the CJ, which lasted from 1954 to 1986.

1996 Rounded headlights

signal the new Wrangler, brought out early for the 1997 model year. It has a stiffer chassis, coil-sprung suspension and an improved interior with air bags.

UNDER THE SKIN

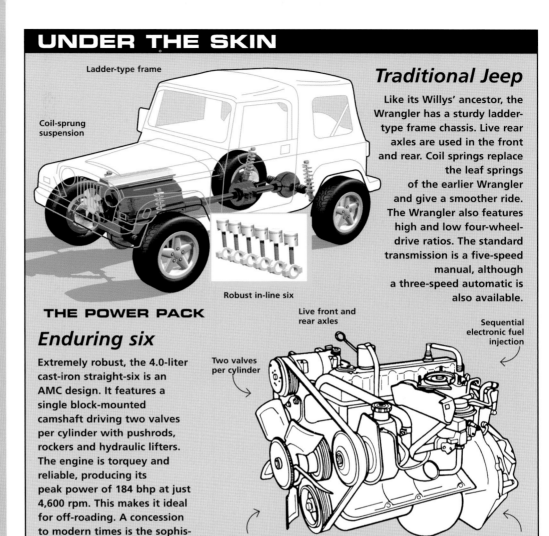

Ladder-type frame

Coil-sprung suspension

Robust in-line six

Traditional Jeep

Like its Willys' ancestor, the Wrangler has a sturdy ladder-type frame chassis. Live rear axles are used in the front and rear. Coil springs replace the leaf springs of the earlier Wrangler and give a smoother ride. The Wrangler also features high and low four-wheel-drive ratios. The standard transmission is a five-speed manual, although a three-speed automatic is also available.

THE POWER PACK

Enduring six

Extremely robust, the 4.0-liter cast-iron straight-six is an AMC design. It features a single block-mounted camshaft driving two valves per cylinder with pushrods, rockers and hydraulic lifters. The engine is torquey and reliable, producing its peak power of 184 bhp at just 4,600 rpm. This makes it ideal for off-roading. A concession to modern times is the sophisticated sequential electronic fuel injection system.

Two valves per cylinder

Live front and rear axles

Sequential electronic fuel injection

Hydraulic valve lifters

Cast-iron block and cylinder head

Super Sahara

The original Jeep has come a long way since 1942. Top of the current range is the Wrangler Sahara, fitted with a 4.0-liter straight-six as standard. It features a deluxe interior and handsome spoked alloy wheels. European Saharas also have full-size doors and come with an optional lift-off hard top.

The latest Wrangler Sahara is refined compared to the previous model.

Jeep WRANGER

Still instantly recognizable, the current Jeep Wrangler has been considerably reworked, both inside and out, resulting in the best all around traditional Jeep ever built.

Part-time four-wheel drive

The Jeep's four-wheel drive system is not permanently engaged like in some 4WD vehicles. It can be selected when required for ice, snow or off-road driving and can be switched in and out of four-wheel and two-wheel drive when the vehicle is moving.

Hard top

A detachable hard top, with glass side and rear windows, plus a rear wiper and a heated rear window, is standard equipment. It is 15 lbs. lighter than the hard top on the old model.

Alloy wheels

Today, many Wranglers are bought as much for image as for their off-road ability. Five-spoke aluminum wheels are standard equipment on the Sahara version.

Disc brakes

The first military Jeeps had four-wheel drum brakes, but the modern vehicles have large discs at the front with drums at the rear.

New bodywork

Although outwardly similar, the current Wrangler shares no body panels with its predecessor, except for the doors. The shape has been softened and round headlights are used again for the first time since 1986. Chrysler has also strengthened the already strong ladder-type frame.

Six-cylinder engine

Wranglers use the same 4.0-liter in-line six-cylinder engine that is also found in the Cherokee. The camshaft profile is conservative and the engine tuned for torque at low rpm for optimal off-road ability.

ENGINE

Type: In-line six

Construction: Cast-iron block and head

Valve gear: Two valves per cylinder operated by one block-mounted camshaft via pushrods, rockers and hydraulic valve lifters

Bore and stroke: 3.88 in. x 3.41 in.

Displacement: 4.0 liter

Compression ratio: 8.75:1

Induction system: Electronic sequential fuel injection

Maximum power: 184 bhp at 4,600 rpm

Maximum torque: 220 lb-ft at 3,600 rpm

Top speed: 112 mph

0–60 mph: 8.8 sec.

TRANSMISSION

Five-speed manual or three-speed automatic with switch-on-the-fly two- or four-wheel drive and high and low ratios

BODY/CHASSIS

Separate ladder-type frame with steel two-door utility body

SPECIAL FEATURES

Factory-fitted tires are, appropriately, Goodyear Wrangler off-roaders.

An automatic transmission is available on the current Wrangler and is ideal for city driving conditions.

RUNNING GEAR

Steering: Recirculating ball

Front suspension: Solid live axle with leading links, coil springs and anti-roll bar

Rear suspension: Solid live axle with four trailing links, coil springs, gas shocks and anti-roll bar

Brakes: Vented discs, 11-in. dia. (front), drums, 9.0-in. dia. (rear)

Wheels: Alloy, 7 x 15 in.

Tires: Goodyear Wrangler 215/75 R15

DIMENSIONS

Length: 152.8 in.   **Width:** 68.1 in.

Height: 70.2 in.   **Wheelbase:** 93.4 in.

Track: 57.9 in. (front and rear)

Weight: 3,349 lbs.

Lamborghini **LM002**

Best known for its supercars, Lamborghini also entered the off-road market with the LM002. This V12-powered monster is the fastest 4x4 vehicle in the world, and also one of the most luxurious and expensive.

"...super off-roader."

"With a big V12 engine up front, the LM002 is terrifyingly quick for such a large vehicle. Push your foot down and the engine howls through the rev range. With so much torque available, the LM002 makes light work of overtaking traffic and yet can still challenge the roughest terrain with ease. Interior fittings are of the highest order, and the high driving position commands respect."

A huge center console dominates the LM002's cabin, leaving less room for passengers than you'd expect.

Milestones

1977 Lamborghini

Hopes to become part of a U.S. military project. The rear-engined Chrysler V8-powered Cheetah is the result and is displayed at the 1977 Geneva Motor Show.

Lamborghini is probably best known for its stunning supercars, like the Diablo.

1985 Although the project

didn't win the U.S. government contract, the Italian vehicle manufacturer presses ahead and presents its LM002 production 4x4 in the autumn.

The LM002 was also fast off-road, and competed in several long-distance rallies.

1993 Lamborghini

announces that the LM002 model will no longer be produced, although there is speculation that the Italian company is working on another off-road vehicle project.

UNDER THE SKIN

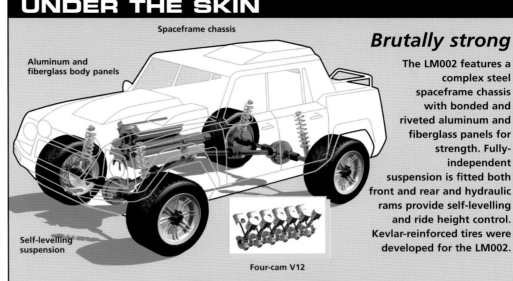

Spaceframe chassis

Aluminum and fiberglass body panels

Self-levelling suspension

Four-cam V12

Brutally strong

The LM002 features a complex steel spaceframe chassis with bonded and riveted aluminum and fiberglass panels for strength. Fully-independent suspension is fitted both front and rear and hydraulic rams provide self-levelling and ride height control. Kevlar-reinforced tires were developed for the LM002.

THE POWER PACK

A supercar V12 engine

The legendary V12 engine from the Countach was dropped into the LM002 in virtually unmodified form, giving 5.2 liters of raw power and torque. It boasts mouth-watering specifications: all-alloy construction and four chain-driven overhead camshafts operating four valves per cylinder. A waterproofed air filter is also fitted for travelling through mud and rivers. For even more power you could order the LM004, which is fitted with a 7.2-liter Lamborghini marine V12 engine producing an enormous 434 lb-ft of torque.

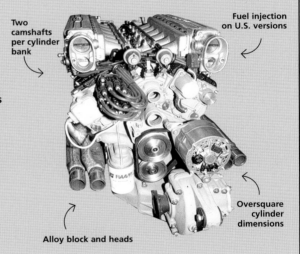

Two camshafts per cylinder bank

Fuel injection on U.S. versions

Oversquare cylinder dimensions

Alloy block and heads

Top dog

There are two models of Lamborghini's incredible 4x4. The entry-level LM002 features a smaller engine. It was the arrival of the much cheaper civilian AM General Hummer which spelled the end for the LM002 and its larger brother, the LM004.

Base model LM002s have a space-aged appearance.

Lamborghini **LM002**

A highly-specialized vehicle which was designed to be the ultimate off-road machine—before the AM General Hummer—the Lamborghini LM002 became the supercar of the 4x4 vehicle market.

Rear load area

The tail-gate opens up to reveal a large rear load area, which can also be used to seat extra passengers—up to six people. This helps to make up for the lack of passenger space inside.

Tough structure

Underneath the aluminum and fiberglass body is a very tough steel chassis clothed in alloy panels. Armor plating was also available as an option.

Supercar engine

The 450-bhp V12 engine offers incredible performance, but has to be mounted high up to maximize ground clearance. Huge fuel tanks are essential for long off-road excursions.

Huge ground clearance

Thanks to the double wishbone suspension, the underside of the LM002 is remarkably free of obstacles. It has 12 inches of ground clearance under each differential.

Luxury interior

Inside, leather trim, plus air-conditioning and power everything is standard.

Specifications

1987 Lamborghini LM002

ENGINE

Type: V12

Construction: Alloy cylinder block and cylinder heads

Valve gear: Four valves per cylinder operated by two overhead camshafts

Bore and stroke: 3.36 in. x 2.95 in.

Displacement: 5,167 cc

Compression ratio: 9.5:1

Induction system: Six Weber twin-choke carburetors

Maximum power: 450 bhp at 6,800 rpm

Maximum torque: 369 lb-ft at 4,500 rpm

Top speed: 126 mph

0–60 mph: 8.5 sec.

TRANSMISSION

Five-speed manual, two-speed transfer case

BODY/CHASSIS

Steel spaceframe with four-door aluminum and fiberglass bodywork

SPECIAL FEATURES

A wide tunnel gives room for a high-mounted engine and transmission.

To cope with the roughest of surfaces, the LM002 has special Kevlar-reinforced tires.

RUNNING GEAR

Steering: Recirculating ball

Front suspension: Double wishbones with coil springs, shocks and anti-roll bar

Rear suspension: Double wishbones with telescopic shocks

Brakes: Discs front, drums rear

Wheels: Optional alloy, 17-in. dia.

Tires: 345/60 VR17

DIMENSIONS

Length: 192.9 in.   **Width:** 78.7 in.

Height: 72.8 in.   **Wheelbase:** 118.1 in.

Track: 63.6 in. (front), 63.6 in. (rear)

Weight: 5,954 lbs.

Land Rover **SERIES 1**

The Jeep paved the way as the standard all-purpose vehicle in WWII; Rover followed by building its own version. Modifying a Willys Jeep chassis, it installed Rover mechanicals. The result was a supreme and effective off-roader.

"...an unbeatable off roader."

"It's the Land Rover's no-nonsense character that appeals to its owners. It's devoid of any sort of frills and everything that is included has a specific and important function. As a result, the Series I Land Rover is an uncomfortable and stark beast. However, the truck's strengths quickly begin to show. The engine is very torquey at a low rpm, and the off-road ability is second to none. For mud-plugging and hill-climbing it is an unbeatable off roader."

Stark and functional, the cabin is not a place for those looking for creature comforts.

Milestones

1947 Land Rover makes its first prototype with a war-surplus Willys Jeep and a Rover engine and transmission.

The work horse was elevated to royal status in 1959, when it was used by Queen and Prince Philip on an official visit.

1948 The Land Rover is launched at the Amsterdam Motor Show. It has an 80-inch wheelbase and uses a 1.6-liter engine.

The modern equivalent of the Series 1 is the Defender.

1951 The headlights are moved from behind the grill and the engine grows to 2.0 liters.

1953 New 86- and 107-inch wheelbase lengths are offered.

1958 The Series 1 gives way to the much improved Series II.

UNDER THE SKIN

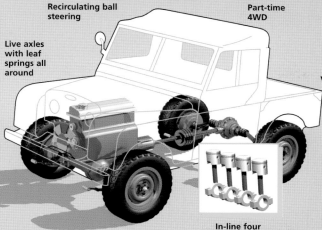

Recirculating ball steering

Part-time 4WD

Live axles with leaf springs all around

In-line four

Jeep-inspired

Rover's chief engineer, Maurice Wilks, happened to be using a Willys Jeep on his Welsh estate when Rover considered building its own agricultural machine. Two war-surplus Jeeps with 80-inch wheelbases were used as prototypes. There was permanent four-wheel drive with free-wheeling front hubs. This system changed in 1950 when the front wheels could be locked and unlocked for four- or two-wheel driving.

THE POWER PACK

Tough Rover engines

Partly to keep costs down and partly because they were tough and therefore ideal for the Land Rover, the Series 1 used a detuned regular production engine from its passenger car range. The first production cars had Rover 60 four-cylinder 1,595-cc engines, with their unusual intake-over-exhaust valve layout. For military use, some 33 trucks were fitted with Rolls-Royce 2.8-liter engines. In 1951, the capacity of the Rover engine was increased to 1,997 cc. This only marginally increased power but boosted torque to 101 lb-ft.

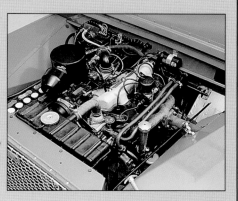

Early to rise

Workhorses are now collectable items, as the Jeep has proved. Here, the maxim is 'the earlier, the better'—collectors prefer the Series I Land Rovers. However, the Series II which debuted in 1958 is bigger, more use-able, less expensive and offered in a greater variety of models. Its basic design lasted until 1983 and its legacy lives on in the current Defender.

Series II Land Rovers came in both short and long wheelbase form.

Land Rover **SERIES 1**

The Series I may have been basic, but it was supposed to be. The Land Rover had to be reliable, easy to service, and able to maintain its go-anywhere reputation. A worldwide legend was very quickly born.

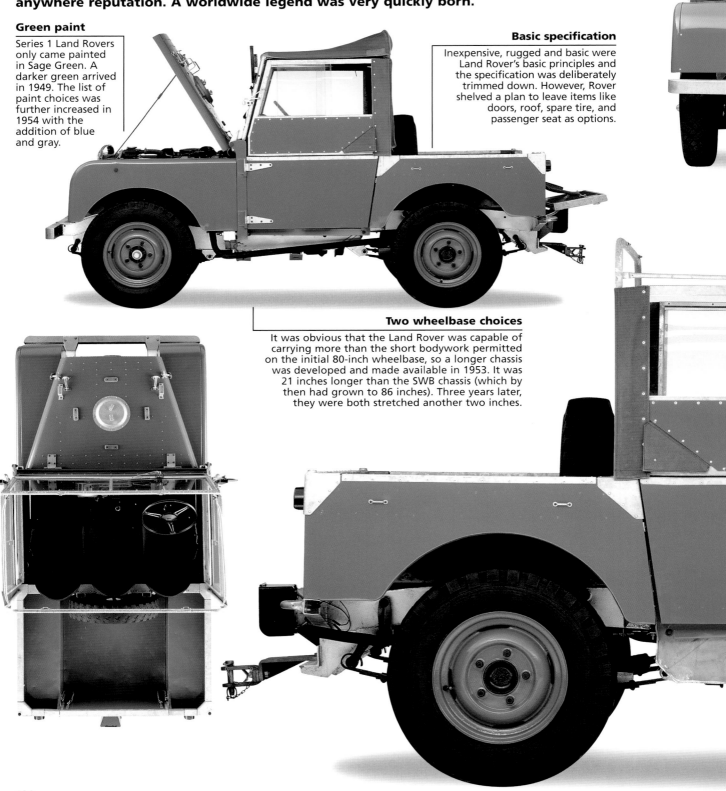

Green paint

Series 1 Land Rovers only came painted in Sage Green. A darker green arrived in 1949. The list of paint choices was further increased in 1954 with the addition of blue and gray.

Basic specification

Inexpensive, rugged and basic were Land Rover's basic principles and the specification was deliberately trimmed down. However, Rover shelved a plan to leave items like doors, roof, spare tire, and passenger seat as options.

Two wheelbase choices

It was obvious that the Land Rover was capable of carrying more than the short bodywork permitted on the initial 80-inch wheelbase, so a longer chassis was developed and made available in 1953. It was 21 inches longer than the SWB chassis (which by then had grown to 86 inches). Three years later, they were both stretched another two inches.

Aluminum bodywork

Shortages of steel in the post-war period forced Rover to adopt aluminum for its bodywork. Although it was more expensive, it was the ideal material—lightweight and easily formed by hand.

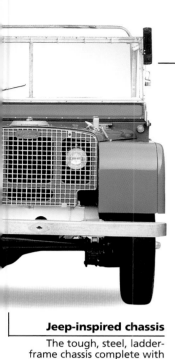

Jeep-inspired chassis

The tough, steel, ladder-frame chassis complete with leaf-sprung rigid axles was clearly developed from the Willys Jeep.

Choice of body styles

Most early Land Rovers were custom made, but there were two basic body styles. The first—and by far the more popular—was an extremely simple pickup with half-doors. The station wagon body with curvaceous paneling was more utilitarian, but not as popular as the pickup.

Specifications

1955 Land Rover Series 1

ENGINE

Type: In-line four-cylinder

Construction: Cast-iron block and head

Valve gear: Two valves per cylinder with intake valve mounted over exhaust valve

Bore and stroke: 3.06 in. x 4.13 in.

Displacement: 1,997 cc

Compression ratio: 6.7:1

Induction system: Single Solex carburetor

Maximum power: 52 bhp at 4,000 rpm

Maximum torque: 101 lb-ft at 1,500 rpm

Top speed: 60 mph

0–60 mph: Not quoted

TRANSMISSION

Four-speed manual with two-speed transfer box

BODY/CHASSIS

Separate chassis with aluminum two-door open body

SPECIAL FEATURES

If the Series 1 can't drive out of a compromising situation, this winch will allow it to pull itself out.

This truck is equipped with these unusual windshield-mounted pop-up turn signals.

RUNNING GEAR

Steering: Recirculating ball

Front suspension: Live axle with semi-elliptic leaf springs and telescopic shock absorbers

Rear suspension: Live axle with semi-elliptic leaf springs and telescopic shock absorbers

Brakes: Drums (front and rear)

Wheels: Steel, 16-in. dia.

Tires: 6.00 x 16

DIMENSIONS

Length: 140.8 in.   **Width:** 62.5 in.

Height: 76.0 in.   **Wheelbase:** 86.0 in.

Track: 50.0 in. (front and rear)

Weight: 2,968 lbs.

Land Rover DEFENDER

First seen in 1948, the classic Land Rover shape continues today as the Defender. Rugged, durable, and able to travel further than almost any off-roader, it has become a legend among four-wheel drive enthusiasts and invaluable to the world's armed forces.

"...Unstoppable in any terrain."

"With its torquey V8 engine, the Defender has the ability to get out of any sticky situation. In the rugged outdoors, the Defender is unstoppable in any terrain. Thanks to its 10 forward gears, lockable differential, superb ground clearance, minimal overhangs, and four-wheel drive, the Defender can climb a 45-degree slope and wade through rivers more than 20 inches deep. The light, damped steering, well-judged springing, and extremely long-travel suspension make light work of deep ruts."

The Defender's interior is very basic, with hard-wearing trim material and a rubber floormat.

Milestones

1948 The first Land Rover is launched with an 80-inch wheelbase, and it is modeled on the Willys Jeep.

1958 In the Series II the four-cylinder engine increases from 2.0 to 2.3 liters.

Series I Land Rovers were extremely basic in specification.

1971 The Series III is fitted with full synchromesh, a new grill, and a safety instrument panel.

1979 The V8 engine becomes an option.

The British Army uses many special versions of the Land Rover.

1985 Restyled Ninety and One-Ten models are built with 90-inch and 110-inch wheelbases.

1990 Revised Defender range is launched, taking the rugged Land Rover toward the end of the millennium.

UNDER THE SKIN

Alloy body

Long-travel coil spring suspension

Sturdy separate steel chassis

Four-cylinder turbodiesel

Old-school toughness

The Defender's chassis may be an old design, but it is extremely tough and has proven itself in many arduous situations. The hefty steel box-section chassis is mated with aluminum body panels. Traditionally, Land Rovers had leaf-sprung suspension, but this has been replaced by coil springs, which increase suspension travel and give a more comfortable ride.

THE POWER PACK

V8 or turbodiesel

There is a choice of engines for the Defender. Rover's venerable all-alloy, ex-Buick V8 has given sterling service in the Land Rover. The engine is lightweight, compact and could produce 182 bhp, but it is tuned for maximum torque rather than outright power. For many customers the four-cylinder, 113-bhp 2.5-liter turbodiesel engine is the preferred choice because it is economical and has immense torque.

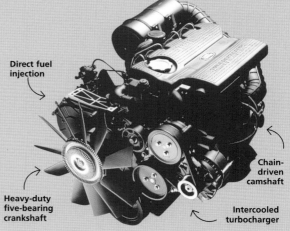

Direct fuel injection

Chain-driven camshaft

Heavy-duty five-bearing crankshaft

Intercooled turbocharger

Short and sweet

The Defender is built in two wheelbase lengths—90 inch and 110 inch. The 90-inch version, powered by a V8 engine, is the better model as it is lighter, and has improved off-road performance. Even in this short version, the station wagon body can seat up to seven people comfortably.

The 90-inch Defender 90 powered with a V8 is one tough off-road vehicle.

Land Rover DEFENDER

This is the quintessential, go-anywhere, no-nonsense off-roader. It may appear utilitarian when compared with the more recent sports-utility competition, but for pure ability the Defender is hard to beat.

Overhang

Minimal front and rear body overhang are essential for climbing ability. The Defender is capable of an approach angle of 48 degrees, along with a departure angle of 45 degrees.

Aluminum body

For light weight, the very stiff bodywork is made of aluminum. All of the panels can be easily replaced if they become damaged. The aluminum body is also more resistant to corrosion than steel.

Ground clearance

With 8.3 inches of ground clearance, the Defender can clear most obstacles in its path. All major components are well protected and electrical equipment is waterproofed, allowing the Defender to splash through rivers up to 20 inches deep.

Seating for seven

Up to seven people can be carried in the Defender 90—three up front and four in the back. The longer wheelbase Defender 110 model can seat nine.

Coil-sprung axles

Live axles front and rear are both rugged and adaptable. For many years the Land Rover suffered from its very stiff leaf springs, but now it has coil springs and telescopic shocks all around.

Turbodiesel power

The older V8 gives better performance but has much higher fuel consumption than the four-cylinder turbodiesel engine. In addition, the turbodiesel achieves maximum torque at a very low 1,800 rpm.

Specifications
1997 Land Rover Defender 90 TDi

ENGINE
Type: In-line four-cylinder turbodiesel
Construction: Iron cylinder block and alloy head
Valve gear: Two valves per cylinder operated by a single overhead camshaft
Bore and stroke: 3.56 in. x 3.81 in.
Displacement: 2,500 cc
Compression ratio: 19.5:1
Induction system: Direct fuel injection with intercooler and turbocharger
Maximum power: 113 bhp at 4,000 rpm
Maximum torque: 194 lb-ft at 1,800 rpm
Top speed: 87 mph
0–60 mph: 13.5 sec.

TRANSMISSION
Five-speed manual with transfer case

BODY/CHASSIS
Aluminum three-door body on steel chassis

SPECIAL FEATURES

The second shifter engages low ratio for rugged off-road driving.

Flip-down steps allow easy access to the extremely high driver's cab.

RUNNING GEAR
Steering: Worm-and-roller
Front suspension: Live axle with coil springs and shocks
Rear suspension: Live axle with coil springs and shocks
Brakes: Discs (front and rear)
Wheels: Steel, 16-in. dia.
Tires: BF Goodrich All-Terrain 205/R16

DIMENSIONS
Length: 157.1 in.   **Width:** 70.5 in.
Height: 80.2 in.   **Wheelbase:** 92.9 in.
Track: 58.5 in. (front), 58.5 in. (rear)
Weight: 3,737 lbs.

Land Rover FREELANDER

This British firm has always produced tough, go-anywhere off-roaders—real all-terrain machines. The Freelander is Land Rover's first move into a crossover market where fun road cars and off-roaders join up. It is smaller than other Land Rovers but has proved just as popular.

"...extremely accomplished."

"The Freelander's natural habitat is suburban streets, and in this role it is extremely accomplished. The performance is perfectly adequate, if not exciting, while the handling is hardly distinguishable from a very good road car—you just roll more because of the higher center of gravity. Off road the Freelander struggles to climb steep slopes since there is no low-speed transfer case, but in most respects it copes admirably."

The Freelander is more traditional inside than some of its rivals.

Milestones

1997 The Freelander
makes its international debut at the September Frankfurt Motor Show.

1997 In October, the car appears
at the British Motor Show at Earl's Court, London.

Land Rovers have been in production since 1948 and are used around the world.

1998 The Freelander first
goes on sale with 1.8-liter gasoline and 2.0-liter diesel engines and as a two- or four-door model. Unlike the larger Discovery, the Freelander is not offered on the U.S. market.

Bigger brother to the Freelander is the high-roof Discovery.

1999 Having proved
a commercial success, the Freelander continues into the new model year with few changes.

UNDER THE SKIN

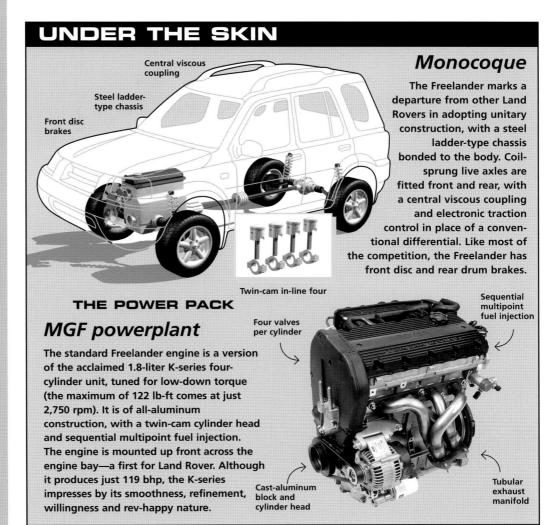

Central viscous coupling

Steel ladder-type chassis

Front disc brakes

Twin-cam in-line four

Monocoque

The Freelander marks a departure from other Land Rovers in adopting unitary construction, with a steel ladder-type chassis bonded to the body. Coil-sprung live axles are fitted front and rear, with a central viscous coupling and electronic traction control in place of a conventional differential. Like most of the competition, the Freelander has front disc and rear drum brakes.

THE POWER PACK

MGF powerplant

The standard Freelander engine is a version of the acclaimed 1.8-liter K-series four-cylinder unit, tuned for low-down torque (the maximum of 122 lb-ft comes at just 2,750 rpm). It is of all-aluminum construction, with a twin-cam cylinder head and sequential multipoint fuel injection. The engine is mounted up front across the engine bay—a first for Land Rover. Although it produces just 119 bhp, the K-series impresses by its smoothness, refinement, willingness and rev-happy nature.

Four valves per cylinder

Sequential multipoint fuel injection

Cast-aluminum block and cylinder head

Tubular exhaust manifold

Stylish softback

Many prefer the 1.8-liter gas engine, but the diesel model is the one to chose if you want torque and fuel economy. The other choice concerns body style, which is up to personal preference. The five-door station wagon is conventionally styled, but the more striking three-door softback has a rear that can operate as an open pickup or as a regular station wagon.

The softback model is the most desirable for young people.

Land Rover **FREELANDER**

The Freelander marks a new generation for Land Rover as a compact sport-utility vehicle. It is enjoyable and capable on the highways as well as off-roading, and with looks that endear it to fashion-conscious buyers.

Side-opening tailgate

The huge rear door opens to the side for easy access. Extra interior space is freed up by mounting the spare wheel on the tailgate. The power rear window drops downward.

Conventional transmission

Unlike other Land Rovers, which have two-speed transfer boxes, the Freelander relies on a normal five-speed transmission. To compensate slightly for the lack of low-speed transfer ratios, it has a low 3.25:1 first gear ratio and a very low axle ratio of 4.20:1.

Unitary construction

Unlike any other Land Rover, the Freelander has an integral body/chassis construction. The substantial steel ladder-type chassis is just grafted onto the body. This saves weight yet keeps the structure very strong and rigid for long-term fit and durability.

Electronic traction control

The ETC system uses the anti-lock braking mechanism to apply braking force to a wheel that is losing traction. At the same time, torque is fed to the wheel on the opposite side to give traction in slippery conditions.

'Intelligent' four-wheel drive

Off-roaders must have permanent four-wheel drive, but the Freelander does without a center differential to join the front and rear drives. Instead it incorporates a central viscous coupling that, combined with electronic traction control, leads Land Rover to claim that this is an intelligent all-wheel drive system.

Trendy styling

To appeal to a younger generation of buyers, the Freelander was styled by Gerry McGovern of MGF fame. The shape attempts to mate an image of solidity with sporty elements such as the steep A-pillars and rounded fenders.

Specifications

1998 Land Rover Freelander 1.8i

ENGINE

Type: In-line four-cylinder

Construction: Aluminum block and head

Valve gear: Four valves per cylinder operated by twin overhead camshafts

Bore and stroke: 3.15 in. x 3.51 in.

Displacement: 1,796 cc

Compression ratio: 9.5:1

Induction system: Sequential multipoint fuel injection

Maximum power: 119 bhp at 5,550 rpm

Maximum torque: 122 lb-ft at 2,750 rpm

Top speed: 108 mph

0–60 mph: 10.5 sec.

TRANSMISSION

Five-speed manual

BODY/CHASSIS

A monocoque configuration with a steel five-door station wagon style body

SPECIAL FEATURES

The bumper-mounted grill contains a filter to prevent ingestion of dirt.

The spare wheel mounting also incorporates the third brake light.

RUNNING GEAR

Steering: Rack-and-pinion

Front suspension: MacPherson struts with lower arms, coil springs and telescopic shock absorbers

Rear suspension: MacPherson struts with trapezoidal link, coil springs and telescopic shock absorbers

Brakes: Discs (front), drums (rear)

Wheels: Steel, 15-in. dia.

Tires: 195/80 HR15

DIMENSIONS

Length: 172.2 in.   **Width:** 81.6 in.

Height: 69.2 in.   **Wheelbase:** 100.6 in.

Track: 60.4 in. (front), 60.8 in. (rear)

Weight: 3,088 lbs.

Land Rover RANGE ROVER

Nothing less than a masterstroke, the Range Rover was the world's first luxury 4x4 vehicle. As well as being one of the most capable off-roaders ever seen, it boasted a high-quality ride, a practical interior and luxurious equipment. It remained the one to beat for the next two decades.

"...excellent 4x4 performance."

"The driving qualities of the Range Rover really sold it to the public, because it's just as happy on the road as it is off it. The torquey V8 engine provides enough pull for excellent 4x4 performance and also enables it to cruise happily at 90 mph. The ride is superb, thanks to compliant coil springs and damping all around. On difficult surfaces the Range Rover has virtually no peers. It can climb steep hills and handle impossibly slippery surfaces."

The inside of the Range Rover is more suited to dress shoes than muddy boots.

Milestones

1970 A truly innovative
new 4x4 vehicle: that's the conclusion of the world's press on the launch of the Range Rover.

The Land Rover was the forerunner to the Range Rover.

1981 A four-door
bodyshell is added to the range.

1985 Fuel injection
and a four-speed automatic arrive.

1986 A 2.4-liter turbo-diesel
engine joins the V8 powerplant.

The new Range Rover, which made its debut in 1994, had a tough act to follow.

1987 The Range Rover
goes on sale in the U.S. and proves an instant hit.

1994 An all-new Range Rover
is launched, but the old model continues in production for one more year as the Range Rover Classic.

UNDER THE SKIN

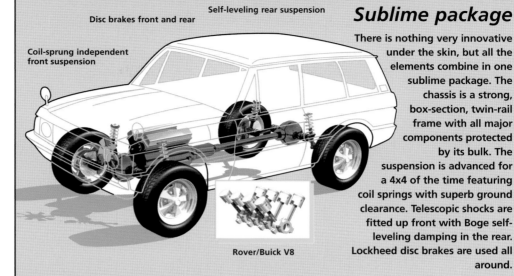

Self-leveling rear suspension

Disc brakes front and rear

Coil-sprung independent front suspension

Rover/Buick V8

Sublime package

There is nothing very innovative under the skin, but all the elements combine in one sublime package. The chassis is a strong, box-section, twin-rail frame with all major components protected by its bulk. The suspension is advanced for a 4x4 of the time featuring coil springs with superb ground clearance. Telescopic shocks are fitted up front with Boge self-leveling damping in the rear. Lockheed disc brakes are used all around.

THE POWER PACK

Eternal V8

The venerable V8 engine used in the Range Rover is a development of the Buick unit used in the 1963 Skylark, then used by Rover in the P5. It was adopted as the ideal powerplant for the Range Rover: compact, very lightweight and torquey. Over the years it has seen a number of developments, including the addition of fuel injection and gradual capacity increases to 4.6 liters that is still used in the current evolution. Diesel options were available.

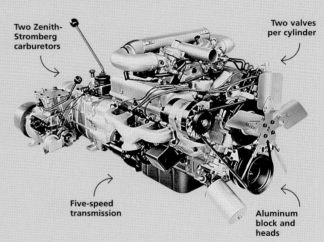

Two Zenith-Stromberg carburetors

Two valves per cylinder

Five-speed transmission

Aluminum block and heads

001 testbed

The Range Rover featured is chassis number 001. Virtually handbuilt before official production started, the car was used as a testbed for components. Found in a barn, it has been meticulously restored to the original spec, including an authentic tool kit.

The off-road ability of the Range Rover was unmatched by its rivals.

Land Rover **RANGE ROVER**

The surprising thing about the Range Rover is not that it was voted the best 4x4 in the world by numerous magazines, but that it was still winning such awards more than 20 years after it was launched.

V8 engine

A detuned (low-compression) version of the perennial Rover/Buick V8 engine powers the Range Rover. Its lightness allows excellent weight distribution and its power and torque are perfect for its intended role.

Live floating axles

Both axles are live and floating, mainly for reasons of ground-clearance and simplicity. Coil springs are fitted front and rear, with Woodhead shocks up front and a Boge Hydromat self-leveling damper strut at the rear. This is because, although the Range Rover has perfect 50:50 weight distribution, the rear end, in some cases, sagged under heavy loads.

Permanent four-wheel drive

Unlike the Land Rover, the four-wheel drive system is permanently engaged, with a special Salisbury differential eliminating windup. The two-speed transfer gear shares the same casing as the main transmission, with a large difference between high and low speeds (2.83 to 1).

Luxurious feel

Compared to the 4x4 standards of its day, this was a very luxurious truck. Although the first Range Rovers had PVC trim and rubber floormats, the seats were well padded and there was an attractive, well-laid-out dash. As the years passed, the Range Rover grew steadily more luxurious, gaining leather upholstery, wood trim, air conditioning, air suspension and so on.

Excellent ground clearance

The lowest point on the Range Rover sits 7 inches above the ground, well out of the way of rocks and ruts. Most of the vulnerable components, such as the transmission and fuel tank, are situated well within the chassis frame for protection. The suspension itself is fairly soft, with up to 8 inches of travel.

Specifications

1970 Land Rover Range Rover

ENGINE

Type: V8

Construction: Aluminum block and heads

Valve gear: Two valves per cylinder operated by a single camshaft with pushrods and rockers

Bore and stroke: 3.50 in. x 2.80 in.

Displacement: 3,528 cc

Compression ratio: 8.5:1

Induction system: Two Zenith-Stromberg carburetors

Maximum power: 130 bhp at 5,000 rpm

Maximum torque: 205 lb-ft at 3,000 rpm

Top speed: 99 mph

0–60 mph: 12.9 sec.

TRANSMISSION

Four-speed manual driving all four wheels

BODY/CHASSIS

Separate chassis with steel and aluminum two-door station wagon body

SPECIAL FEATURES

Early Range Rovers came with a simple four-speed transmission as standard.

The V8 engine was detuned to optimize off-road performance.

RUNNING GEAR

Steering: Recirculating-ball

Front suspension: Live axle with leading arms, Panhard rod, coil springs and shock absorbers

Rear suspension: Live axle with A-bracket, radius arms, self-leveling strut, coil springs and shock absorbers

Brakes: Discs (front and rear)

Wheels: Steel, 16-in. dia.

Tires: 205 x 16

DIMENSIONS

Length: 176.0 in.   **Width:** 70.0 in.

Height: 70.0 in.   **Wheelbase:** 100.0 in.

Track: 58.5 in. (front and rear)

Weight: 3,864 lbs.

Range Rover OVERFINCH

The Range Rover is the king of luxury off-roaders, as happy acting as a limousine as tackling the rough stuff. But specialists Overfinch take it several steps further, installing a powerful GM 5.7-liter V8 engine and uprating the rest of the SUV to match.

"...performance edge."

"You buy an Overfinch for its performance edge, so as soon as you bury the accelerator, the uprated V8 instantly delivers its punch. The power is applied safely by the sophisticated four-wheel drive transmission, and there's a solid wall of performance up to very high speeds. Ultimately, the poor aerodynamics get in the way of top speed, which stands at around 130 mph. But it's the sheer torque available that's most impressive."

This Overfinch's interior has been color-keyed to match the outside.

Milestones

1975 Under the name Schuler,
Overfinch creates its first modified Range Rover.

Overfinch has been modifying Range Rovers for nearly 25 years.

1982 The 570T is launched,
Overfinch's first-ever Chevy V8-powered Range Rover.

1990 With fuel injection,
the model is renamed 570 TPi (Tuned Port Injection).

Overfinch will also modify the smaller Land Rover Discovery.

1995 A very special and limited
20th Anniversary model is produced with a 380-bhp 6.8-liter GM V8.

1998 For the first time,
Overfinch tackles the all-new Range Rover SE and HSE, converting these under the name 570 SE and 570 HSE.

UNDER THE SKIN

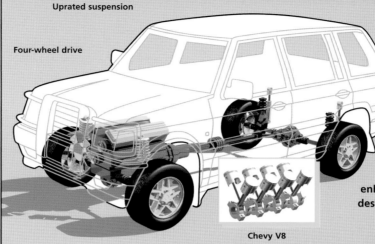

Uprated suspension

Four-wheel drive

Chevy V8

Not just brute force

Making a sportier Range Rover isn't just a case of giving it more power. Overfinch looked at the whole vehicle to provide a satisfactory all-around performer. There is an enhanced suspension layout designed to reduce the sport utility's body roll and to improve body control on undulating surfaces.

THE POWER PACK

GM small block V8

Overfinch replaces the ex-Buick V8 with an even bigger engine: the classic GM 5.7-liter small block V8 engine. In Overfinch form it has a tuned-length induction system, multi-point fuel injection, fully-mapped ignition, an advanced engine management system, cast-aluminum low friction pistons, aluminum heads, high swirl combustion chambers, twin high-flow catalysts, free-flow headers and an uprated cooling system. The result is a reliable, efficient engine capable of 330 bhp.

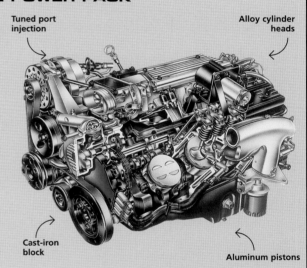

Tuned port injection

Alloy cylinder heads

Cast-iron block

Aluminum pistons

Luxury express

For people who think that a Range Rover isn't luxurious enough and are let down by a lack of power, than an Overfinch conversion is perfect. All of the strengths of the original Range Rover are kept, but the modifications create a fast and luxurious express SUV.

Overfinch Range Rover—the world's best off-roader?

Range Rover OVERFINCH

If your Range Rover isn't fast enough, then go to Overfinch; they will transform the vehicle into something that is superior in every respect, much like what AMG will do with a Mercedes or Alpina with a BMW.

Subtle body styling

One of the most attractive aspects of the Overfinch is that it looks almost identical to the regular Range Rover. Painting this example in Ferrari Giallo Fly yellow makes it stand out.

GM V8 engine

Overfinch takes a 5.7-liter V8 engine from General Motors, modifies it to suit and puts it in the Range Rover engine bay. Performance is greatly enhanced, as power jumps to 330 bhp and torque goes up to a massive 425 lb-ft.

Bentley tires

To enhance on-road performance, Overfinch specifies Avon Turbospeed WR-rated tires, the same as those used by Bentley.

Seven seats

The standard Range Rover has five seats, but Overfinch produces a clever seven-seater conversion. There is a third row of seats arranged as a rear-facing bench, which can be folded up flat against the seat back.

Quicker steering

With a steering ratio some 20 percent quicker than normal, the Overfinch's responses are more akin to a sports car than an off-roader. It does mean that extra care needs to be taken off road.

Enhanced suspension

The basics of the live axle suspension are retained, but there are tweaks to firm up the air control system that comes as standard on the Range Rover HSE. The result is much sharper handling response.

Front end modifications

The nose is the most modified in cosmetic terms. It features a color-coded bumper and grill and a wraparound nudge bar.

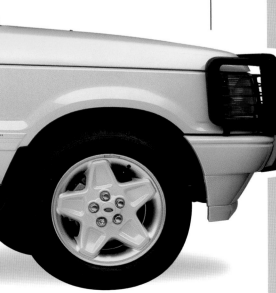

Specifications

1998 Overfinch 570 HSE

ENGINE

Type: V8

Construction: Cast-iron block and aluminum heads

Valve gear: Two valves per cylinder operated by single camshaft via pushrods and rockers

Bore and stroke: 4.0 in. x 3.48 in.

Displacement: 5,733 cc

Compression ratio: 10:1

Induction system: Fuel injection

Maximum power: 330 bhp at 4,700 rpm

Maximum torque: 425 lb ft at 3,150 rpm

Top speed: 130 mph

0–60 mph: 7.2 sec.

TRANSMISSION

Four-speed automatic

BODY/CHASSIS

Separate chassis with four-door aluminum station wagon body

SPECIAL FEATURES

Convenient rear-facing extra rear seats fold away when not in use.

A hefty nudge bar gives extra protection for the headlights.

RUNNING GEAR

Steering: Recirculating ball

Front suspension: Live axle with longitudinal arms, Panhard rod, air springs and telescopic shock absorbers

Rear suspension: Rigid axle with longitudinal arms, Panhard rod, air springs and telescopic shock absorbers

Brakes: Discs (front and rear)

Wheels: Alloy 16-in. dia.

Tires: 255/60 WR16

DIMENSIONS

Length: 185.5 in. **Width:** 73.0 in.

Height: 71.6 in. **Wheelbase:** 108.1 in.

Track: 60.6 in. (front), 60.2 in. (rear)

Weight: 4,960 lbs.

Lincoln **NAVIGATOR**

With the boom in upscale sport-utility vehicles, Ford decided it wanted a slice of the market. Enter the Navigator, an F-series based off-roader with a powerful 5.4-liter 230-bhp V8 engine and luxury interior appointments.

"...does the driving for you."

"Sitting in a Navigator is much like getting behind the wheel of a Lincoln Town Car, though the high driving position offers a better view of the road. Off the highway, the Navigator is surprisingly capable. Select low range four-wheel drive and the vehicle rises an inch higher at speeds under 25 mph, helping it clear difficult obstacles. On the highway, the Navigator is relaxing to drive, being quite comfortable and refined."

A spacious interior offers power everything and standard leather upholstery.

Milestones

1996 The last of the F-150-based two-door Bronco off-roaders goes on sale.

Mercury launched its first sport utility, the Mountaineer, in 1997.

1997 Ford launches its first full-size four-door sport-utility vehicle, the Expedition. Based on the new 1997 F-150, it is designed to compete with the Chevrolet Tahoe and has selectable four-wheel drive.

The Navigator is based on the full-size Ford Expedtition.

1998 Lincoln introduces an upscaled version of the Ford Expedition. Called the Navigator, it has styling touches to differentiate it from lesser models, a standard 5.4-liter V8 and a luxury interior. It is available in two- or four-wheel drive and can tow up to 8,000 lbs.

UNDER THE SKIN

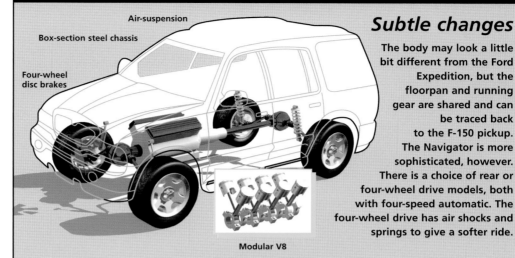

Air-suspension

Box-section steel chassis

Four-wheel disc brakes

Modular V8

Subtle changes

The body may look a little bit different from the Ford Expedition, but the floorpan and running gear are shared and can be traced back to the F-150 pickup. The Navigator is more sophisticated, however. There is a choice of rear or four-wheel drive models, both with four-speed automatic. The four-wheel drive has air shocks and springs to give a softer ride.

THE POWER PACK

High-tech V8

All Navigators use the 5.4-liter Triton version of Ford's modular V8 engine. Although it is a cast-iron engine with two valves per cylinder, it has a single overhead camshaft per bank and sequential multi-point electronic fuel injection. It produces a stump-pulling 325 lb-ft at a low 3,000 rpm, allowing the Navigator to scramble over rough terrain with ease. The modular V8 also has platinum-tipped spark plugs which will last for 100,000 miles.

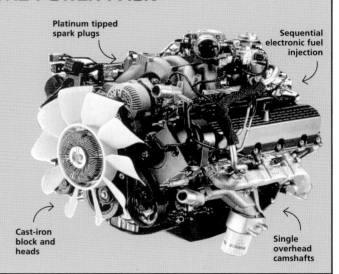

Platinum tipped spark plugs

Sequential electronic fuel injection

Cast-iron block and heads

Single overhead camshafts

Better buy

Although a two-wheel drive version is available, the four-wheel drive model is the better choice. It costs just over $3,000 more, but it is far more tractable and easier to drive. Off-road, the 4WD version will handle itself in just about any terrain.

Navigators have one of the highest towing capacities of any off-roader.

Lincoln **NAVIGATOR**

Equally at home in the most elegant of residential areas, roaming through a national park or towing a power boat, the Navigator is the most versatile vehicle Lincoln has ever built.

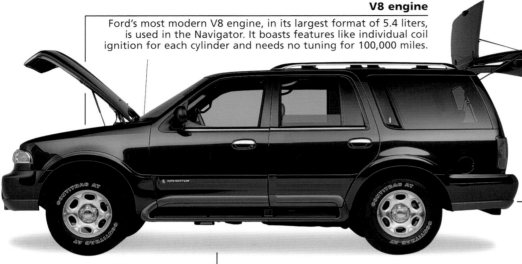

V8 engine

Ford's most modern V8 engine, in its largest format of 5.4 liters, is used in the Navigator. It boasts features like individual coil ignition for each cylinder and needs no tuning for 100,000 miles.

Skid plates

The Navigator is the only Lincoln ever made to need skid plates. They are fitted under the vehicle to prevent damage to engine or transmission when the Navigator goes off road.

Live rear axle

The one area in which the Navigator shows its Ford F-150 truck chassis origins is the live rear axle. It is well located, however, with upper and lower trailing arms and a Panhard rod to prevent lateral movement.

Four-speed automatic

The only transmission available is Ford's four-speed overdrive automatic with a column-mounted shift lever.

Rear tailgate

For extra convenience the rear tailgate is split so that either the upper glass section or the whole door can be opened depending on the size of the load.

Air suspension

Like the Lincoln Mk VIII coupe, air springs are are used on all four wheels of the 4WD Navigator. They work in conjunction with the automatic load leveling facility which senses the load and adjusts the suspension pressure accordingly.

Speed sensitive steering

Although old-fashioned, a recirculating ball steering system is used on this Lincoln. It's allied to speed-sensitive power assistance.

Illuminated running boards

To save knocked or bruised shins and the sort of undignified stumbles quite inappropriate to a Lincoln owner, the running boards are illuminated at night when the doors are unlocked.

Perfect accommodation

Not only do the power front seats have a memoryfunction with three settings but there are bucket seats for the second row of passengers and a bench seat for the third row. All seats can be leather trimmed if desired and the third-row bench can be removed for extra luggage space.

Specifications

1998 Lincoln Navigator

ENGINE

Type: V8

Construction: Cast iron block and alloy heads

Valve gear: Two valves per cylinder operated by single overhead cam per bank of cylinders

Bore and stroke: 3.55 in. x 4.16 in.

Displacement: 5.4 liter

Compression ratio: 9.0:1

Induction system: Multi-port sequential fuel injection

Maximum power: 230 bhp at 4,250 rpm

Maximum torque: 325 lb-ft at 3,000 rpm

Top speed: 109 mph

0–60 mph: 11.4 sec.

TRANSMISSION

Four-speed auto with four-wheel drive, high and low ratio

BODY/CHASSIS

Separate box section frame with steel SUV four-door seven- or eight-passenger body

SPECIAL FEATURES

High-intensity headlights give excellent illumination at night.

Directional arrows appear in the mirrors at night when the indicators are in use.

RUNNING GEAR

Steering: Recirculating ball

Front suspension: Double wishbones with air springs and anti-roll bar

Rear suspension: Live axle with air springs, trailing arms, Panhard rod and anti-roll bar

Brakes: Vented discs, (front), solid discs, (rear), ABS standard

Wheels: alloy, 7.5 in. x 17 in.

Tires: P255/75R 17

DIMENSIONS

Length: 204.8 in.   **Width:** 79.9 in.

Height: 76.7 in.   **Wheelbase:** 119 in.

Track: 65.4 in. (front), 65.5 in. (rear)

Weight: 5,557 lbs.

Mercedes-Benz ML320

After many years of struggling along with the antiquated G-Wagon, Mercedes-Benz has created an exciting new car for the lucrative recreational SUV market. The ML320 is one of the best available.

"...on-road refinement."

"After the old G-Wagon, the M-class is a revelation. It has been designed with on-road refinement as much in mind as off-road capability. For an SUV, it moves along pretty well. The ride is good, with the coil-sprung suspension soaking up bumps. Off road, the unconventional, four-wheel drive system proves to be effective although it falls short of traditional off-road setups."

Compared to its predecessor, the M-class is more like a luxury sedan with all the vital instruments right in front of the driver.

Milestones

1979 The G-Wagon
4x4 is introduced and is Mercedes-Benz's only 4x4 model until 1997.

Although likely to be used mainly on road, the ML320 is very capable off road, too.

1993 Mercedes-
Benz executives begin discussing the development of a sports utility vehicle. It is decided that the new vehicle should be built at a new factory in America, making it the first U.S.-built Mercedes.

The ML320 is built in a new factory in Tuscaloosa, Alabama.

1997 After nearly
four years of development, the ML320 makes its debut in September. With a new engine and increased occupant protection, it is the most efficient and safest SUV on the market.

UNDER THE SKIN

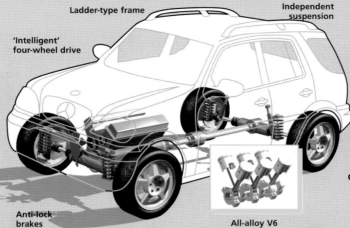

Ladder-type frame

Independent suspension

'Intelligent' four-wheel drive

Anti-lock brakes

All-alloy V6

Rugged chassis

A tough box-section ladder-type frame plus all-independent suspension allows the ML320 to tackle virtually any terrain and makes it fun to drive. Braking is provided by four-wheel discs. A brake-operated traction-control system ensures the ML320 doesn't get stuck in the mud.

THE POWER PACK

Low emissions

For its brand-new truck, Mercedes also designed a new engine. The 3.2-liter all-alloy V6 has twin spark plugs, three valves per cylinder—the exhaust valves are sodium-filled—to ensure that it satisfies California's ultra-stringent low emissions standards. It produces 215 bhp and 233 lb-ft of torque, providing excellent on-road performance and good mud-plugging ability. Because it is based on a V8 engine, there is a balancer shaft that reduces vibration.

Sodium-filled exhaust valves

90° V6 layout

Counter rotating balancer shaft

Three valves per cylinder

Upmarket

Currently, the ML320 is only available with a V6-powered engine. Its name is sure to attract upmarket SUV buyers, while the 3.2-liter engine gives good performance both on and off road. A 4.3-liter V8 model is scheduled to join the line up soon.

Softer lines make the M-class more appealing to non-truck buyers.

Mercedes-Benz ML320

Built at a new factory in Alabama, the ML320 is one of the first sport utility vehicles (SUVs) to try to combine the best features of both a car and a truck.

Powerful V6 engine

A brand-new engine had to be designed to fit in the engine bay. The 3.2-liter V6 is one of the most powerful units in its class.

Spacious interior

Effective use of space was a major factor in the design. The ML320 can seat up to seven people, and can carry more luggage than the Ford Explorer.

Independent suspension

A notable feature for an SUV is the all-independent suspension set-up, which improves both the handling and the ride.

Dual-mode ABS

Anti-lock brakes are standard and feature a special dual mode that minimizes stopping distances under certain conditions.

ETS four-wheel drive system

A special four-wheel drive system employs two open differentials. If the system detects a loss of traction to one wheel it applies brake pressure to it, hence forcing more traction to the other tires.

Deformable fuel tank

The fuel tank is housed inside the frame rails. The filler neck is specially designed to prevent it from being ripped from its mounting during a collision.

Occupant protection

The ML320 is a pioneer of SUV safety, being fitted with door-mounted airbags and pyrotechnic seat belt pretensioners.

Ground clearance

Nothing, apart from the lower wishbones, protrudes lower than 8.4 inches above the road. The fuel tank, exhaust, and front differential are protected by crossmembers.

Specifications

1998 Mercedes-Benz ML320

ENGINE

Type: V6

Construction: All-alloy block and heads

Valve gear: Three valves per cylinder operated by a single camshaft per bank

Bore and stroke: 3.53 in. x 3.3 in.

Displacement: 3,199 cc

Compression ratio: 10.0:1

Induction system: Sequential electronic fuel injection

Maximum power: 215 bhp at 5,500 rpm

Maximum torque: 233 lb-ft at 3,000 rpm

Top speed: 112 mph

0–60 mph: 8.9 sec.

TRANSMISSION

Five-speed automatic

BODY/CHASSIS

All-steel body on separate box frame

SPECIAL FEATURES

The use of three valves per cylinder helps to increase power and to reduce emissions.

High-intensity headlights aid visibility at night and give the ML320 a distinctive frontal aspect.

RUNNING GEAR

Steering: Power-assisted rack-and-pinion

Front suspension: Double wishbones with torsion bar, telescopic shock absorbers, and anti-roll bar

Rear suspension: Double wishbones with coil springs, telescopic shock absorbers, and anti-roll bar

Brakes: Vented discs (front and rear)

Wheels: Cast-aluminum, 8.0 x 16 in.

Tires: Dunlop Grandtrek 255/65/TR16

DIMENSIONS

Length: 180.6 in.   **Width:** 72.2 in.

Height: 69.9 in.   **Wheelbase:** 111 in.

Track: 60.4 in. (front and rear)

Weight: 4,200 lbs.

Mitsubishi **MONTERO SPORT**

With the Montero Sport, Mitsubishi offers a downsized version of its existing full-size SUV. There's still the advantage of shift-on-the-fly, four-wheel drive and V6 power, but in a more manageable package.

"...traction is impressive."

"It feels immensely solid and well put together, but that doesn't mean it's slow. Even though it takes more than 10 seconds to reach 60 mph, it has a sporting flavor not found in many other SUVs. On the road it's fine, with only moderate understeer, a good ride and very effective all-disc brakes. Off-road, the steering feels more at home; with the low ratio engaged in four-wheel drive combined with the optional limited-slip differential, traction is impressive."

All the Montero's instruments are models of clarity, and equipment levels are generous.

Milestones

1988 The Montero name makes
its debut on Mitsubishi's large sport utility, which is tough, unsophisticated and ideal off-road.

The Shogun is the Montero's bigger brother.

1992 For the 1993 model year,
Mitsubishi revamps the Montero. The base engine is the 151-bhp, 3.0-liter V6. By the late 1990s, the only engine is a 3.5-liter V6 with 200 bhp and a four-speed automatic.

In other markets, the Montero Sport is called the Challenger.

1997 Mitsubishi launches
a U.S. version of its L-200 to broaden the Montero range. The new model is the Montero Sport, which is shorter and lower than the full-size model. It comes with engines ranging from a base 2.4-liter rear drive, through V6 options. Top of the model range is the Limited.

UNDER THE SKIN

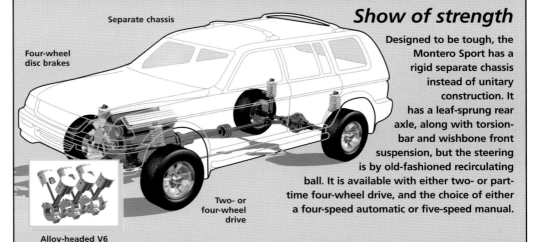

Separate chassis

Four-wheel disc brakes

Two- or four-wheel drive

Alloy-headed V6

Show of strength

Designed to be tough, the Montero Sport has a rigid separate chassis instead of unitary construction. It has a leaf-sprung rear axle, along with torsion-bar and wishbone front suspension, but the steering is by old-fashioned recirculating ball. It is available with either two- or part-time four-wheel drive, and the choice of either a four-speed automatic or five-speed manual.

THE POWER PACK

Tough but refined

SUVs now have engines that are just as advanced as cars'. In this case, it is Mitsubishi's iron-block and alloy-headed V6. The unit is a short-stroke, free-revving 3.0-liter V6 with a single overhead camshaft per bank of cylinders, but it still uses four valves per cylinder. The valves are opened via hydraulic valve lifters, which are used to promote low maintenance and quiet running. The four-valve nature shows in the engine speed at which maximum torque is produced. It comes fairly high up at 4,000 rpm, in contrast to the traditional off-road requirement that engines produce low lugging power.

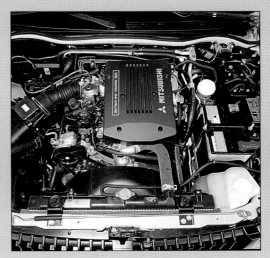

ES option

If you're not going off-road, the Sport ES might well be the best bet. It still has the 173-bhp V6 but uses rear-wheel drive only, which helps cut a huge amount of weight. As a result, the ES has a very clear performance edge over the off-roader.

Sport ES models are lighter than four-wheel-drive versions, and so are quicker.

Mitsubishi **MONTERO SPORT**

In the extremely competitive U.S. SUV market, you need more than just ability to succeed. The Montero Sport has that in abundance, but it also has outstanding good looks to help it attract buyers.

Selectable four-wheel drive

On some four-wheel drive vehicles the driver has to come to a halt before switching the truck in or out of four-wheel drive. But in the Montero Sport the driver can shift change from two- to four-wheel drive at speed.

V6 engine

The more powerful versions of the Montero Sport have the 3.0-liter V6 engine. It is very oversquare with a short stroke, and a wide bore allows room for the four valves per cylinder, which allow it to breath better.

Live rear axle

There are off-roaders and SUVs with independent rear suspension, but Mitsubishi—along with popular off-road kings Jeep and Land Rover—persist with a new live axle.

Separate chassis

There is a lot of pickup truck technology in the Montero Sport. Under the stylish body is a traditional ladder frame with two main chassis rails running fore and aft, onto which the body is attached. That makes the construction heavier than a unitary body, but it is very strong.

Torsion-bar suspension

There are packaging advantages to using longitudinal torsion bars at the front—they do not interfere with the driveshafts. Changing the shock absorbers is also easier if they are not mounted concentrically in a coil spring.

Alloy wheels

Although steel wheels are standard, the Montero Sport can be ordered with alloy wheels. It is part of the premium package, which also includes a leather steering wheel and power windows as well as running boards.

Specifications

1998 Mitsubishi Montero Sport XLS

ENGINE
Type: V6

Construction: Cast-iron block and alloy heads

Valve gear: Four valves per cylinder operated by a single belt-driven overhead camshaft per bank of cylinders

Bore and stroke: 3.59 in. x 2.99 in.

Displacement: 2,972 cc

Compression ratio: 9.0:1

Induction system: Electronic fuel injection

Maximum power: 173 bhp at 5,250 rpm

Maximum torque: 188 lb-ft at 4,000 rpm

Top speed: 105 mph

0–60 mph: 10.1 sec.

TRANSMISSION
Five-speed manual or four-speed automatic

BODY/CHASSIS
Separate steel ladder-frame chassis with steel SUV body

SPECIAL FEATURES

The vast majority of Montero Sports are sold with automatic transmissions.

Discreet but clear badging distinguishes the Sport model.

RUNNING GEAR
Steering: Recirculating ball

Front suspension: Double wishbones with torsion bars, telescopic shock absorbers and anti-roll bar

Rear suspension: Live axle with semi-elliptic leaf springs, telescopic shock absorbers and anti-roll bar

Brakes: Vented discs, 10.8-in. dia. (front), drums, 10.6-in. dia. (rear)

Wheels: Alloy, 6 x 15 in.

Tires: 265/70 R15

DIMENSIONS
Length: 178.3 in.   **Width:** 66.7 in.

Height: 65.6 in.   **Wheelbase:** 107.3 in.

Track: 57.7 in. (front), 58.3 in. (rear)

Weight: 3,985 lbs.

Saleen **EXPLORER**

Having produced some of the fastest Mustangs in the world, Steve Saleen's company has turned its attentions to the Explorer SUV, giving it on-road performance to match its off-road ability.

SALEEN *EXPLORER*

"...prepare to be amazed."

"Hop from an ordinary Explorer to a Saleen-modified variant and prepare to be amazed. Gone is the vague handling, replaced by much quicker responding steering and stiffer bushings. Because it has larger diameter anti-roll bars and a lowered suspension, there's no lag between what you want the car to do and what it does. Saleen's modifications show in the ride, too. Despite a stiffer setup, it rides better, thanks to revalved shocks."

Bucket seats give the interior a decidedly sporty feel.

Milestones

1990 Ford's new SUV, the Explorer, is unveiled early in January at the Los Angles and Detroit Auto Shows. Originally there's only one engine available, the 4.0-liter pushrod V6.

Saleen also produced the red-hot S351 Mustang for IMSA racing.

1996 The Explorer gets the welcome addition of a V8 engine. It's the 5.0-liter pushrod V8 giving 210 bhp.

The standard Explorer has itself seen a number of modifications.

1998 Steve Saleen's company takes the V8 version, now with 215 bhp standard, and transforms it into the high-performance Saleen Explorer.

1999 For 1999, new colors are added to the Explorer range and Saleen offers chrome wheels.

UNDER THE SKIN

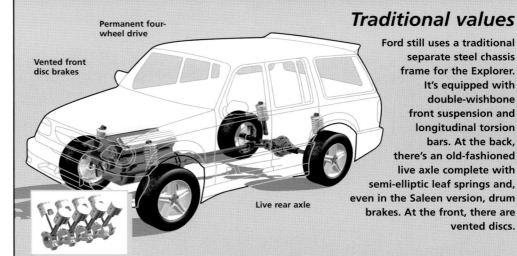

Permanent four-wheel drive

Vented front disc brakes

Supercharged V8

Live rear axle

Traditional values

Ford still uses a traditional separate steel chassis frame for the Explorer. It's equipped with double-wishbone front suspension and longitudinal torsion bars. At the back, there's an old-fashioned live axle complete with semi-elliptic leaf springs and, even in the Saleen version, drum brakes. At the front, there are vented discs.

THE POWER PACK

Serious boost

Saleen improves all three engine options in the Explorer with simple modifications to give a freer-flowing exhaust and air cleaner. Top of the list is the V8 with optional mechanically driven supercharger rather than an exhaust-driven turbo. Otherwise, there's the familiar Ford 5.0-liter pushrod V8 with its short stroke, two valves per cylinder and hydraulic valve lifters. In standard form, that originally put out 210 bhp at 4,600 rpm, but the addition of the blower sends that up to 286 bhp.

Two less

Even the 'base' model Saleen Explorer is an impressive performer. Saleen's modifications increase the V6's output to 211 bhp. It's better balanced than the larger V8 models and still decently fast, easily capable of running 16.2-second ¼ mile times.

V6 models offer a good compromise between performance and cost.

169

Saleen **EXPLORER**

An Explorer that handles and can run the ¼-mile quicker than most cars? The Saleen version does all this and more. Best of all, it is guaranteed to make you stand out from the crowd.

Rear wing

Helping keep the back of the Explorer firmly located, Saleen adds a rear wing to provide downforce at high speed. It's there for added style as well.

Lower ride height

Improving handling on-road, where this Explorer will spend most of its time, Saleen lowers the ride height by two inches. On a skidpad, it generates 0.80 g of lateral grip.

Body modifications

The look of the Explorer is transformed by Saleen's body modifications, consisting of urethane rocker panel extensions, front fascia and rear valance.

Uprated suspension

Saleen's suspension improvements consist of shorter springs, stiffer and thicker front and rear anti-roll bars and harder urethane anti-roll bar bushings. Revalved shock absorbers are also fitted.

170

Revised hood

Helping make this extra-special Explorer stand out from the pack and provide better engine cooling, Saleen fits a new hood, incorporating twin functional scoops. This is similar in design to the one seen on the S351 Mustang.

Uprated exhaust

Saleen's tuning improvements to the V6 and V8 engines include an open-element air filter, but more important, the mufflers and exhaust pipes are replaced with a free-flowing system.

V8 engine

In 1996, the Explorer was finally given a V8 engine. For its top performer, Saleen adds a mechanically driven supercharger and extracts an extra 76 bhp.

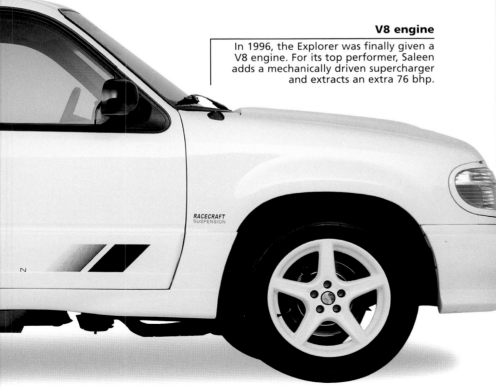

RACECRAFT SUSPENSION

Specifications

1998 Saleen Explorer

ENGINE

Type: V8

Construction: Cast-iron block and heads

Valve gear: Two valves per cylinder operated by single camshaft with pushrods and rocker arms

Bore and stroke: 4.0 in. x 3.0 in.

Displacement: 302 c.i.

Compression ratio: 9.0:1

Induction system: Electronic fuel injection

Maximum power: 286 bhp at 4,500 rpm

Maximum torque: 333 lb-ft at 3,200 rpm

Top speed: 125 mph

0–60 mph: 7.9 sec.

TRANSMISSION

Four-speed automatic

BODY/CHASSIS

Separate ladder frame with steel SUV body

SPECIAL FEATURES

Vents in the rear bumper have become a trademark of Saleen vehicles.

The rear windows on all explorers can be opened separately for quick access.

RUNNING GEAR

Steering: Recirculating ball

Front suspension: Double wishbones with longitudinal torsion bars, telescopic shock absorbers and anti-roll bar

Rear suspension: Live axle with semi-elliptic leaf springs, telescopic shock absorbers and anti-roll bar

Brakes: Vented discs (front), drums (rear)

Wheels: Magnesium, 8.5 x 18 in.

Tires: Pirelli Scorpion II HR M+S, 255/55 R18

DIMENSIONS

Length: 188.5 in.   **Width:** 70.6 in.

Height: 65.7 in.   **Wheelbase:** 111.5 in.

Track: 59.0 in. (front), 59.0 in. (rear)

Weight: 4,500 lbs.

Shelby **DAKOTA**

Introduced in 1987, the Dakota was one of the first mid-size pickups to uncover a substantial market. With the boom in hot trucks in the late 1980s, Carroll Shelby decided to build a limited-production Dakota.

"...first-rate performance."

"It may feel somewhat dated today, but the Shelby-modified Dakota has plenty of interior space. However, space efficiency is the last reason you would want to own one of these sporty trucks. With a torquey 318 V8 and short gearing, this truck sprints off the line to 60 mph in less than 9.0 seconds. With Shelby's track experience, this truck offers first- rate performance and commendable handling. Furthermore, its precise steering is in a league of its own."

Full instrumentation, including a 6,000-rpm tachometer, tells you this is no average truck.

Milestones

1986 Replacing the Mitsubishi-derived

Ram 50 is the new home-grown Dakota. Bigger than rival compact trucks, it comes with a standard 3.9-liter V6 and is available in two- or four-wheel drive.

Shelby's entry-level vehicle in 1989 was the Dodge Shadow-based CSX subcompact.

1989 A sport model is added

to the range, with blackout trim, cast-aluminum wheels and a 125-bhp, 3.9-liter V6. Carroll Shelby decides to build a hotter version and squeezes a 5.2-liter V8 into the engine bay. Handling suspension, performance tires and graphics highlight the Shelby Dakota. Projected output is 1,500 units per year.

Second-generation Dakotas have either 5.2- or 5.9-liter V8s.

1991 A V8 becomes available on

the regular Dakota, which also receives a new nose.

UNDER THE SKIN

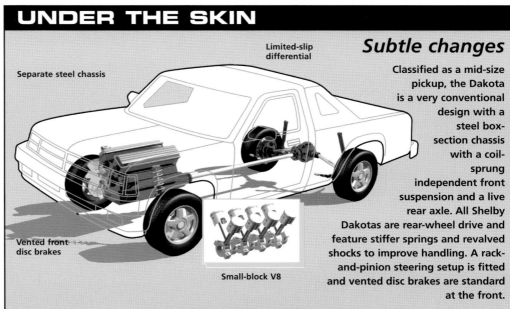

Limited-slip differential

Separate steel chassis

Vented front disc brakes

Small-block V8

Subtle changes

Classified as a mid-size pickup, the Dakota is a very conventional design with a steel box-section chassis with a coil-sprung independent front suspension and a live rear axle. All Shelby Dakotas are rear-wheel drive and feature stiffer springs and revalved shocks to improve handling. A rack-and-pinion steering setup is fitted and vented disc brakes are standard at the front.

THE POWER PACK

Veteran V8

Early first generation Dakotas came stock with rather anemic 3.9-liter V6s, but Shelby decided that his new truck needed a V8 engine. The 318-cubic inch, small-block V8 available in the full-size Ram seemed ideal for the job. This cast-iron V8 was veteran technology by the 1980s, but could still meet emissions requirements and was incredibly easy to tune. The only modification required for installation in the Dakota was replacing the stock fan with twin electric units, primarily for clearance reasons. With 175 bhp and 270 lb-ft of torque, Shelby Dakotas could run 16.5-second ¼-mile elapsed times.

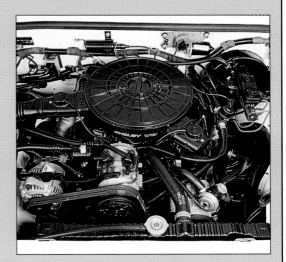

Balancing act

Among hot trucks from the late 1980s and early 1990s, the Shelby Dakota is one of the best balanced. It may not be as quick as current sport trucks, but it is still fun to drive and limited production ensures it will be a future collectable.

Shelby Dakotas were sold through 100 select dealers.

Shelby DAKOTA

With the growing popularity of customized trucks for leisure use, Carroll Shelby saw an opportunity to market a hot version of the mid-size Dakota, complete with full warranty and dealer backup.

Small-block V8

Dropping the 318-cubic inch V8 into the Dakota Sport transformed the truck into a serious performer. The only modification required was substituting the engine-driven fan for two electric ones. A bonus was an extra 5 bhp and improved cooling efficiency.

Performance rubber

A set of Goodyear Eagle GT+4 tires helps improve handling and traction. These were some of the best tires available at the time and were also used on Chrysler's police vehicles.

Heavy-duty suspension

Even though it is quick in a straight line, the Shelby is also designed for excellent handling, too. Stiffer springs and revalved shocks help improve cornering. The Shelby is capable of 0.81 lateral g, which is quite remarkable for a truck.

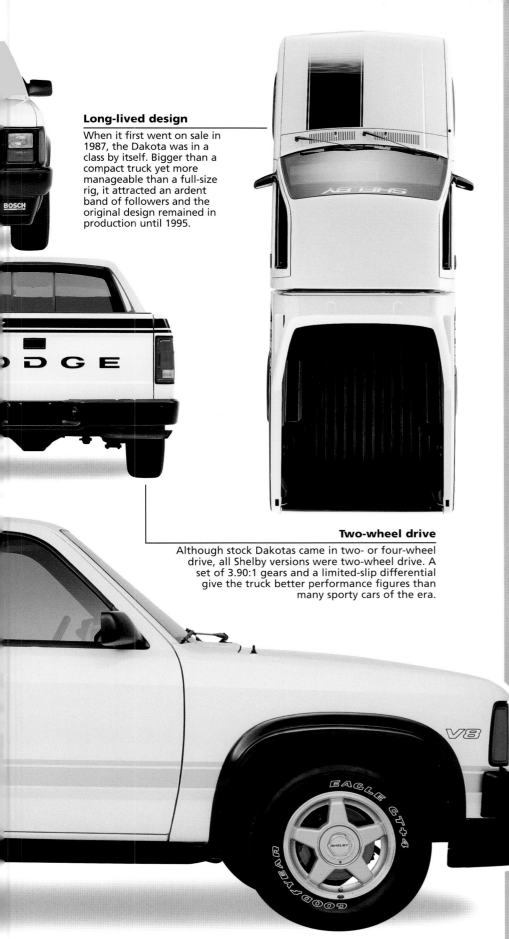

Long-lived design

When it first went on sale in 1987, the Dakota was in a class by itself. Bigger than a compact truck yet more manageable than a full-size rig, it attracted an ardent band of followers and the original design remained in production until 1995.

Two-wheel drive

Although stock Dakotas came in two- or four-wheel drive, all Shelby versions were two-wheel drive. A set of 3.90:1 gears and a limited-slip differential give the truck better performance figures than many sporty cars of the era.

Specifications

1989 Shelby Dakota

ENGINE

Type: V8

Construction: Cast-iron block and heads

Valve gear: Two valves per cylinder operated by a single centrally mounted camshaft with pushrods and rockers

Bore and stroke: 3.91 in. x 3.31 in.

Displacement: 318 c.i.

Compression ratio: Not quoted

Induction system: Carter Thermoquad four-barrel downdraft carburetor

Maximum power: 175 bhp at 4,000 rpm

Maximum torque: 270 lb-ft at 2,000 rpm

Top speed: 175 mph

0–60 mph: 8.5 sec.

TRANSMISSION

Four-speed automatic

BODY/CHASSIS

Steel chassis with steel cab and pickup box

SPECIAL FEATURES

To further exploit the Shelby Dakota's handling, Goodyear Eagle GT+4 tires were fitted.

A sports bar behind the cab enhances the appearance but adds no strength to the body's structure.

RUNNING GEAR

Steering: Rack-and-pinion

Front suspension: Upper and lower wishbones with coil springs, telescopic shock absorbers and anti-roll bar

Rear suspension: Live axle with semi-elliptic leaf springs and telescopic shock absorbers

Brakes: Discs (front), drums (rear)

Wheels: Cast aluminum, 6 x 15

Tires: Goodyear Eagle GT+4, P255/75 HR15

DIMENSIONS

Length: 189.9 in.   **Width:** 73.9 in.

Height: 66.9 in.   **Wheelbase:** 112.0 in.

Track: 59.3 in. (front and rear)

Weight: 3,610 lbs.

Shelby **S.P.360**

In stock form, the Durango is a class-leading SUV, with a powerful V8 engine and unbeatable towing capacity. Turning it into the awesome S.P. 360 results in a truck that has few peers.

"...sheer opulence."

"The first thing that strikes you when you climb into the S.P. 360 is the sheer opulence of the cabin—this is a rig conceived to transport its occupants in absolute luxury. The sound of the supercharger after you have turned the key is a hint of the performance on command. Planting your right foot to the floor brings a rush of acceleration. A completely reworked suspension also enables the driver to tackle corners with confidence."

Bucket seats, CD changer and plenty of wood elevate the S.P. to ultra-luxury status.

Milestones

1995 A new Dakota makes its debut as a 1996 model.
It adopts the styling cues of its big brother, the Dodge Ram, and proves instantly popular. Powertrain choices are expanded to include a 3.9-liter V6, 5.2- and 5.9-liter Magnum V8 engines. The Dakota is the only domestic mid-size pickup.

Shelby's first 'muscle truck' was the 1989 Shelby Dakota.

1997 The new Durango Sport
Utility is based on the Dakota. It shares powertrains, chassis and suspension with its pickup sibling and likewise proves a success.

Launched in 1997, the Durango is a consistent sales champion.

1998 On October 4th,
the first Shelby S.P. 360 is revealed as a hot-rod version of the Durango. Only 3,000 copies are slated for the 1999 model year.

UNDER THE SKIN

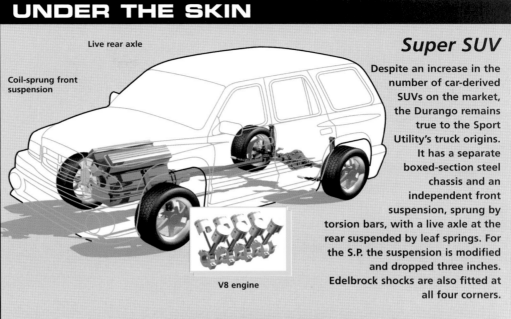

Live rear axle

Coil-sprung front suspension

V8 engine

Super SUV
Despite an increase in the number of car-derived SUVs on the market, the Durango remains true to the Sport Utility's truck origins. It has a separate boxed-section steel chassis and an independent front suspension, sprung by torsion bars, with a live axle at the rear suspended by leaf springs. For the S.P. the suspension is modified and dropped three inches. Edelbrock shocks are also fitted at all four corners.

THE POWER PACK

Extra power
Standard in the regular Durango is a 3.9-liter V6, though most buyers specify the bigger 5.2- and 5.9-liter V8s. The latter, with 245 bhp, gives this fairly heavy SUV excellent sprinting ability, but there are those who seek still more. For them, Shelby and Performance West deliver. The S.P. 360 gets a Kenne Bell 2,200 Blowzilla with up to 13 psi of boost, an Optimizer CPU, a Ram Air induction kit, and a pair of Kenne Bell Extractor equal-length exhaust headers. These upgrades are enough to bump power from 250 to a whopping 360 bhp and also take torque from 335 to 414 lb-ft.

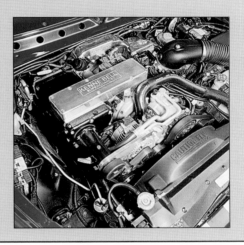

Limited build
With an allocated production run of just 3,000 units for 1999, the Shelby Durango is destined to be a collectible vehicle. At the moment, however, it is an immensely fun-to-drive and fairly practical SUV with head-turning looks.

All 1999 S.P. 360s are painted in Viper Blue with white stripes.

Shelby S.P.360

As SUVs have risen in popularity, so has the aftermarket dedicated to upgrading them. The 1999 Shelby S.P. 360 is perhaps the most shining example of a new breed of ultra-fast, ultra-luxurious sport utilities.

Supercharged V8

Bolting a supercharger, Ram Air system and headers on the 5.9-liter Magnum results in a truly formidable powerplant, with 360 bhp and 414 lb-ft of torque.

GPS system

Most S.P. 360s are loaded to the gills and feature a TV, video and stereo system, plus a Global Positioning System, which pinpoints the Durango's exact location by satellite.

Reworked suspension

One of the stock Durango's strongest attributes is its ground clearance, enabling it to clear all but the roughest terrain. One of the S.P. 360's strongest points, however, is its handling, thanks to the lowered (by three inches) and reengineered suspension, with modified camber, caster and recalibrated springs and steering.

Four-wheel disc brakes

One major improvement over the stock Durango is in the braking department. Big cross-drilled discs and four-piston calipers at the front translate into a sizeable decrease in stopping distance.

Single paint choice

In keeping with recent Dodge-based performance vehicles, such as the Viper GTS and Ram VTS pickup, the 1999 S.P. 360 is sprayed in Viper Blue, with twin white stripes covering the hood, roof and rear. No other colors are available on the 1999 model.

Performance exhaust

No hot-rod vehicle is complete without a performance exhaust, and this applies to the S.P., which has a Kenne Bell stainless steel cat-back dual system.

Specifications

1999 Shelby S.P. 360

ENGINE

Type: V8

Construction: Cast-iron block and heads

Valve gear: Two valves per cylinder operated by a single V-mounted camshaft with pushrods and rockers

Bore and stroke: 4.0 in. x 3.58 in.

Displacement: 360 c.i.

Compression ratio: 8.9:1

Induction system: Sequential multipoint fuel injection

Maximum power: 360 bhp at 4,000 rpm

Maximum torque: 414 lb-ft at 3,200 rpm

Top speed: 132 mph

0–60 mph: 6.4 sec.

TRANSMISSION

Four-speed overdrive automatic

BODY/CHASSIS

Separate steel chassis with four-door station wagon body

SPECIAL FEATURES

Kenne-Bell supplied the dual chromed exhaust tips, which protrude through the rear valance.

A variety of different seating layouts are available, including this six-bucket seat arrangement.

RUNNING GEAR

Steering: Recirculating-ball

Front suspension: Upper and lower A-arms, longitudinal torsion bars, telescopic shock absorbers and anti-roll bar

Rear suspension: Live axle, semi-elliptic leaf springs and telescopic shock absorbers

Brakes: Discs (front and rear)

Wheels: Daytona alloy 18 x 8 in.

Tires: Goodyear F1 GS 295/45 ZR18

DIMENSIONS

Length: 193.3 in. **Width:** 72.4 in.

Height: 69.9 in. **Wheelbase:** 115.9 in.

Track: 63.0 in.

Weight: 4,515 lbs.

Toyota **LAND CRUISER**

Land cruisers have been around for almost 50 years, but there has never been one like the latest model with its advanced V8 engine, luxury fittings and tremendous off-road ability.

"...it feels all-conquering."

"The combination of precise rack-and-pinion steering and new wishbone front suspension produces a Landcruiser which feels much more at home on the road than the previous model. You sit high up, with a commanding view, and automatically-adjusting shocks give an extremely comfortable ride. The quad-cam V8 has the punch to really move the Toyota forward. Off road, it feels as all-conquering and indestructible as ever."

The upmarket Landcruiser Amazon includes leather upholstery and plenty of gadgets.

Milestones

1980 In production since 1955, the Landcruiser is now available with a six-cylinder diesel engine, high and low four-wheel drive and front disc brakes.

1988 The Landcruiser Mk II, with a smaller, turbocharged 85 bhp, 2.5-liter diesel engine, is launched.

Earlier Landcruisers were much more angular. This is a short-wheelbase model.

1992 A completely reworked full-size Landcruiser appears. It is available with larger 4.2-liter straight-six gas and diesel engines.

1996 The Landcruiser is joined by a smaller version, the Colorado, which has two or four doors.

Toyota's entry-level SUV is the sporty RAV-4.

1998 Another fully reworked big Landcruiser is now offered with a V8 engine.

UNDER THE SKIN

Smoother riding

Toyota has improved the Landcruiser by switching from a solid front axle to independent suspension with double wishbones for better on-road comfort and longer suspension travel off road. There is permanent four-wheel drive, with lockable center and rear differentials, as well as the usual high and low ratios, automatic ride height control and even automatically-adjusting shock absorbers.

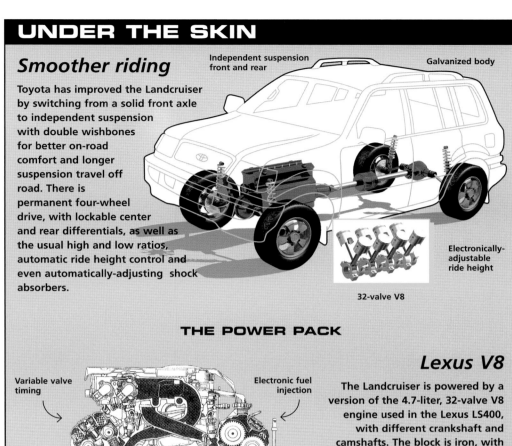

Independent suspension front and rear

Galvanized body

Electronically-adjustable ride height

32-valve V8

THE POWER PACK

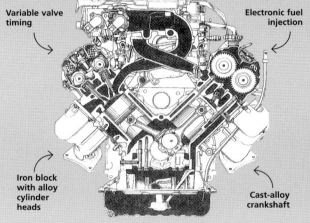

Variable valve timing

Electronic fuel injection

Iron block with alloy cylinder heads

Cast-alloy crankshaft

Lexus V8

The Landcruiser is powered by a version of the 4.7-liter, 32-valve V8 engine used in the Lexus LS400, with different crankshaft and camshafts. The block is iron, with alloy heads and four belt-driven camshafts. Variable valve timing is used in the exhaust rather than inside the engine, and is operated by exhaust pressure which helps to ensure that 90 percent of maximum torque is available from as low as 2,000 rpm. In the big Landcruiser, the V8 produces 232 bhp and 320 lb-ft of torque.

Good value

Although only offered with a 4.2-liter straight-six engine, the previous generation of Landcruisers are worth a look. Immensely tough, they can tackle anything and are more reliable and better value than many other sport utility vehicles.

The current Land Cruiser is a well-equipped and very capable off-roader.

Toyota **LANDCRUISER**

The Landcruiser deservedly reigns supreme in some of the world's toughest off-road markets, and now it has the sophistication to compete around town as well.

Adaptive suspension

Shock absorber settings are speed sensitive; the faster the Landcruiser goes the stiffer the shock absorbers become to improve control. Alternatively, the driver can override the system and chose one of four settings, from comfort to sport.

Ride height adjustment

To make getting in and out easier, the ride height can be lowered. Above 3 mph it lifts itself into the 'Normal' driving position. For rough ground the 'High' setting can be selected.

Rust protection

To combat rust, galvanized steel is used for the floorpan, doors, wheel cutouts and front inner section of the vehicle. Outer panels, including the rear tailgate, are zinc/iron-plated steel.

Lockable differentials

The center differential automatically locks when the driver shifts into low ratio. In high ratio, locking is manual via a switch on the center console. A locking rear differential, which is available as an option, provides even more grip.

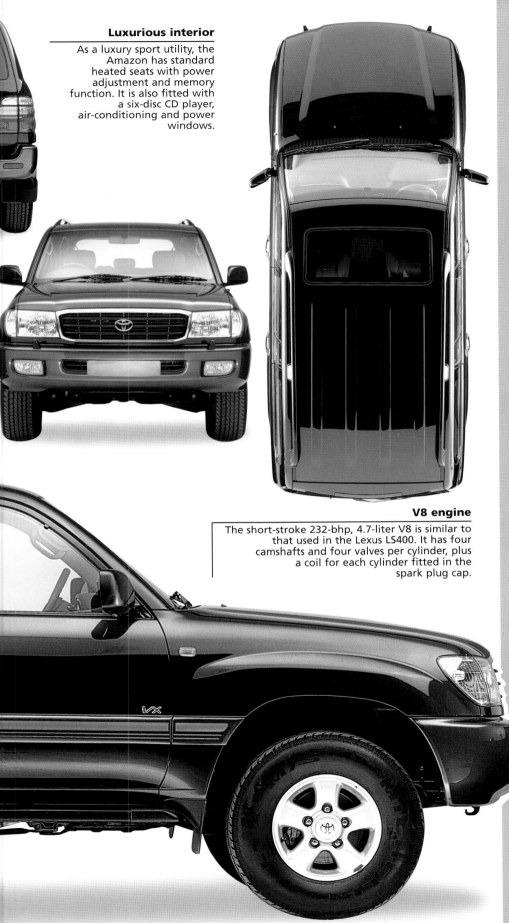

Luxurious interior
As a luxury sport utility, the Amazon has standard heated seats with power adjustment and memory function. It is also fitted with a six-disc CD player, air-conditioning and power windows.

V8 engine
The short-stroke 232-bhp, 4.7-liter V8 is similar to that used in the Lexus LS400. It has four camshafts and four valves per cylinder, plus a coil for each cylinder fitted in the spark plug cap.

Specifications

1998 Toyota Landcruiser Amazon

ENGINE
Type: V8

Construction: Cast-iron block and alloy heads

Valve gear: Four valves per cylinder operated by four belt-driven overhead camshafts

Bore and stroke: 3.7 in. x 3.3 in.

Displacement: 4,664 cc

Compression ratio: 9.6:1

Induction system: Electronic fuel injection

Maximum power: 232 bhp at 4,800 rpm

Maximum torque: 320 lb-ft at 3,400 rpm

Top speed: 109 mph

0–60 mph: 9.9 sec.

TRANSMISSION
Four-speed automatic with permanent four-wheel drive, high and low ratio and lockable center differential

BODY/CHASSIS
Frame-reinforced, high-strength steel, sport utility, four-door, seven-seater body

SPECIAL FEATURES

Huge five-spoke alloy wheels look stylish and are also tough for handling off-road conditions.

Amazon models have extra inward-facing seats, to accommodate more passengers.

RUNNING GEAR
Steering: Rack-and-pinion

Front suspension: Double wishbones with longitudinal torsion bars and adjustable telescopic shock absorbers

Rear suspension: Live axle with four trailing links, Panhard rod, coil springs and adjustable telescopic shock absorbers

Brakes: Vented discs (front and rear)

Wheels: Alloy, 16-in. dia.

Tires: 275/70 R16

DIMENSIONS
Length: 192.5 in.   **Width:** 76.4 in.

Height: 74.0 in.   **Wheelbase:** 112.2 in.

Track: 63.8 in. (front), 63.6 in. (rear)

Weight: 5,200 lbs.

Volkswagen **BEACH BUGGY**

Although an exceptional form of transport in its own right, the Volkswagen Beetle has also been a popular basis for beach buggies, thanks to its simple construction and an engine that is both easy to service and tune.

"...fun in the sun."

"Conceived primarily for fun-in-the-sun motoring, the VW Beach Buggy offers little in the way of occupant protection. Inside it is pretty spartan, but when you're bouncing through the boonies on a hot summer's day, none of this seems to matter. The VW flat-four, while not immensely powerful, is more than adequate, and the basic suspension and large tires are ideally suited for going over sand dunes. Although it has drums front and rear, braking is still good."

Like the Beetle from which it is derived, this buggy has a plain but functional interior.

Milestones

1938 Dr Ferdinand Porsche builds the first Kdf Wagen.

1945 The first civilian examples finally leave the Wolfsburg factory.

1949 The Beetle is first offered in export markets.

Baja Bugs—Beetles with cutaway bodies and large tires— are another typical beach car.

1953 An oval window replaces the previous split back light.

1954 Engine size is increased to 1,192 cc.

The Meyers Manx is the most imitated buggy in the world.

1962 Californian Bruce Meyers produces the original beach buggy—the Manx—using a fiberglass body on a VW chassis. It is so popular that rivals start to build similar designs.

UNDER THE SKIN

Beetle-based

Like many beach buggies, this stylish example has its origins in the Volkswagen Beetle. Its chassis is a VW backbone unit with a one-inch steel box section welded along the body mounting points to give greater stiffness. The suspension is from the Beetle, too, with ball joint torsion bars. The front units have been lowered by 5 inches using Sway-a-Way adjusters, while the rear units have also been lowered by one spline. Braking is from four-wheel drums.

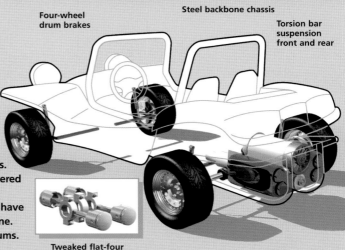

Four-wheel drum brakes

Steel backbone chassis

Torsion bar suspension front and rear

Tweaked flat-four

THE POWER PACK

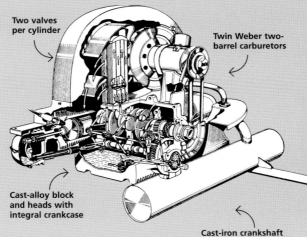

Two valves per cylinder

Twin Weber two-barrel carburetors

Cast-alloy block and heads with integral crankcase

Cast-iron crankshaft

VW bus power

Powering this one-of-a-kind beach buggy is the venerable VW flat-four engine. Developed in the mid-1930s, it has an alloy block with integral crankcase and two cylinders opposing each other. Unlike many other engines, it relies on oil for lubrication and air for cooling. This particular unit, from a 1974 VW bus, is more or less stock, but has been bored out to 1,776 cc and fitted with a high-lift 110-degree cam and twin Weber twin-barrel carburetors for better performance.

Trendsetter

Perhaps the ultimate buggy is the Meyers Manx, built by enterprising Californian Bruce Meyers. It has a fiberglass body bolted onto a shortened VW chassis. Its styling caught on immediately and it became regarded as 'The Beach Buggy.'

Many later beach buggies mimic the style of the Manx.

Volkswagen BEACH BUGGY

This example dates from the golden age of the buggy and oozes 1960s charm with its classic styling and period custom touches like chromed suspension and moon-type chromed aluminum wheels.

Fiberglass body

Most buggies have fiberglass bodies, which were easy and cost-effective to mold in small numbers and had the advantage of keeping weight down, thus enabling ample performance even with small engines. The one-piece unit can be easily lifted off to facilitate servicing.

Modern rubber

Tire technology has come a long way since the 1960s and for greater road holding, safety and grip, this buggy rides on modern tires with Pirelli P700s at the front and meaty Goodyear NCT radials at the rear.

Flat-four engine

Mounted at the rear on a separate subframe, the 1,776-cc engine is of later vintage than the buggy itself and has been tweaked with a high-lift camshaft, larger intake and exhaust valves and drinks fuel from a pair of Weber 40-mm twin-barrel carburetors.

Torsion bar suspension

Like the chassis, the torsion bar suspension, fitted to all models except the 1970-1976 Super Beetles, is rugged and simple. It is also easy to alter the ride height, and the owner of this buggy has done just that, dropping the front by a whopping 5 inches.

Drum brakes

Although many people see drums as antiquated, they are in keeping with the period feel of this buggy. In order to improve braking, the front and rear wheel cylinders have been swapped over, resulting in better balance when the pedal is depressed.

Backbone chassis

One of the major reasons why the VW Beetle is so popular as a basis for buggies is the simple and strong backbone chassis. The floorpans can easily be removed and new bodies fitted.

Specifications

1967 Volkswagen Beach Buggy

ENGINE
Type: Horizontally-opposed four-cylinder
Construction: Alloy block and heads
Valve gear: Two valves per cylinder operated by a single camshaft via pushrods
Bore and stroke: Not quoted
Displacement: 1,776 cc
Compression ratio: 8.5:1
Induction system: Twin Weber two-barrel carburetors
Maximum power: 80 bhp at 4,600 rpm
Maximum torque: 70 lb-ft at 2,300 rpm
Top speed: 98 mph
0–60 mph: 10.2 sec.

TRANSMISSION
Four-speed manual

BODY/CHASSIS
Steel backbone chassis with fiberglass body

SPECIAL FEATURES

Oval-shaped taillights add character to the rear end.

A custom-built subframe holds the engine and is also chromed.

RUNNING GEAR
Steering: Worm and nut
Front suspension: Semi-trailing adjusters, transverse torsion bars with sway adjusters and telescopic shock absorbers
Rear suspension: Swing axles with transverse torsion bars with telescopic shock absorbers
Brakes: Drums (front and rear)
Wheels: Chrome moonshine, 6.0 x 14.0 in. (front), 8.5 x 15.0 in. (rear)
Tires: Pirelli P700z, 185/55 (front), Goodyear NCT, 235/60 x 15 (rear)

DIMENSIONS
Length: 125.5 in.   **Width:** 66.5 in.
Height: 49.0 in.   **Wheelbase:** 90.5 in.
Track: 54.0 in. (front), 57.0 in. (rear)
Weight: 1,190 lbs.

Willys JEEP

There are few motoring institutions so essentially American as the Jeep. Despite the fashionable status of the current Wrangler, the Jeep started out as a U.S. army vehicle during World War II.

"...can tackle any terrain."

"When the world's largest army needed an all-purpose vehicle during World War II, it had to be able to withstand virtually any kind of terrain. There are no frills in the Willys Jeep and it's designed for utility alone. The Jeep feels very solid, with rock-hard suspension and a choppy ride. The steering may be vague, but the torquey engine pulls strong in any gear. This gutsy little four-wheeler really proved its worth for the U.S. Armed Forces."

No creature comforts here. Only the bare essentials are found inside the Jeep.

Milestones

1940 The U.S. Quartermaster Corps

publishes a requirement for a compact 4x4 ¼-ton truck. A design from Bantam is chosen.

1941 Production

begins at the Bantam, Ford, and Willys factories.

Total wartime Jeep production totalled nearly 650,000.

1945 Willys plugs

on with the Jeep in civilian CJ-2A form, while the new Jeep Station Wagon becomes America's first steel-bodied station wagon.

A post-war variation was the 1950 Jeep four-wheel drive pick-up.

1948 A civilian Jeepster

model, with whitewall tires, bright colors, and luxury fittings, is introduced.

1955 The long-running CJ-5 appears. In

1970 Willys is absorbed by AMC.

UNDER THE SKIN

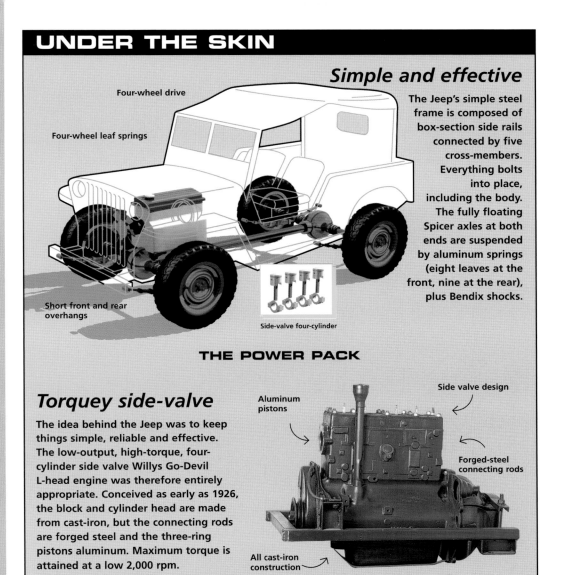

Simple and effective

The Jeep's simple steel frame is composed of box-section side rails connected by five cross-members. Everything bolts into place, including the body. The fully floating Spicer axles at both ends are suspended by aluminum springs (eight leaves at the front, nine at the rear), plus Bendix shocks.

Four-wheel drive

Four-wheel leaf springs

Short front and rear overhangs

Side-valve four-cylinder

THE POWER PACK

Torquey side-valve

The idea behind the Jeep was to keep things simple, reliable and effective. The low-output, high-torque, four-cylinder side valve Willys Go-Devil L-head engine was therefore entirely appropriate. Conceived as early as 1926, the block and cylinder head are made from cast-iron, but the connecting rods are forged steel and the three-ring pistons aluminum. Maximum torque is attained at a low 2,000 rpm.

Aluminum pistons

Side valve design

Forged-steel connecting rods

All cast-iron construction

Many makers

The Willys model is best-known, but this vintage four-wheeler was also built by Bantam (which originally designed the vehicle) and Ford (which badged it as the GPW—hence the name, 'Jeep'). All three are almost identical, although Ford stamped its logo on every component.

The Jeep proved highly adaptable for a variety of roles.

Willys JEEP

Although conceived for wartime use, the Jeep continues to impress today. It is still versatile, effective off-road, simple to work on, and great fun to drive.

Dependable engine

Power comes from a 134 cubic inch, four-cylinder engine producing 60 bhp. A low state of tune ensures excellent reliability.

Under-seat fuel tank

A 15-gallon fuel tank is located under the driver's seat. For the sake of practicality, a gasoline can with an extra 5 gallons' capacity is also attached to the rear.

Storage bins

Just behind each front seat is a locker for tools. A small compartment at the far right of the instrument panel was designed to hold gas masks and goggles.

Basic seating

There is basic seating for four passengers. Seats are filled with cattle hair and rubber (later, springs and felt) and covered with water-resistant cotton.

Simple body

The ultra-simple bodywork of the Jeep is designed for ease of manufacture and repair, and is made of low-carbon steel. A huge variety of Jeeps have been produced, including ambulances, rocket-launchers, staff cars, six-wheelers and even amphibians (dubbed 'Seeps').

Canvas top

Notable for its absence of effective weather protection, the Jeep has a canvas top held in place by two tubular bows; there is no canvas at the sides.

Minimal overhangs

The Jeep still boasts one of the best gradient-climbing abilities of any 4x4 vehicle, being capable of approach and departure angles of up to 45 degrees.

Rugged transmission

There are only three gears, but this is adequate because the engine has enough torque to pull from very low revs. For off-road use there is a two-speed transfer case.

USA
2061857

Specifications
1942 Ford GPW Jeep

ENGINE
Type: In-line four-cylinder
Construction: Cast-iron cylinder block and cylinder head
Valve gear: Pushrod-operated side-valves with single chain-driven camshaft
Bore and stroke: 3.13 in. x 4.37 in.
Displacement: 134 c.i.
Compression ratio: 6.48:1
Induction system: Single Carter downdraft carburetor
Maximum power: 60 bhp at 3,600 rpm
Maximum torque: 105 lb-ft at 2,000 rpm
Top speed: 62 mph
0–60 mph: 30 sec.

TRANSMISSION
Three-speed manual

BODY/CHASSIS
Steel frame with doorless open steel body

SPECIAL FEATURES

Useful items such as spades and axes can be strapped to the bodywork for excursions deep into the country.

Simple in the extreme, early Jeeps lacked a glove compartment but did include a rifle mount.

RUNNING GEAR
Steering: Variable-ratio cam and twin-lever
Front suspension: Spicer floating axle with alloy leaf springs and Bendix hydraulic shock absorbers
Rear suspension: Spicer floating axle with alloy leaf springs and Bendix hydraulic shock absorbers
Brakes: Drums, front and rear
Wheels: Steel split-rim, 16-in. dia.
Tires: 6.00 x 16 in.

DIMENSIONS
Length: 132.3 in.   **Width:** 62 in.
Height: 69 in.   **Wheelbase:** 80 in.
Track: 48.3 in. (front), 43.8 in. (rear)
Weight: 2,453 lbs.

Index